BY-WAY BIKING

in

LANCASHIRE

Henry Tindell

Published by Sigma Leisure – an imprint of Sigma Press, 1 South Oak Lane, Wilmslow, Cheshire SK9 6AR, England.

British Library Cataloguing in Publication Data
A CIP record for this book is available from the British Library.

ISBN: 1-85058-625-X

Typesetting and Design by: Sigma Press, Wilmslow, Cheshire.

Cover photograph: view to a distant Pendle, from the first bridleway, route 8 (Ostwaldtwistle).

Text maps and photographs: Henry Tindell

Printed by: MFP Design and Print

Disclaimer: the information in this book is given in good faith and is believed to be correct at the time of publication. No responsibility is accepted by either the author or publisher for errors or omissions, or for any loss or injury howsoever caused. Only you can judge your own fitness, competence and experience.

Foreword

By Chris Boardman, MBE

Lancastrians have always enjoyed cycling. From Sunday afternoon rides with the family to competitive cycling at the highest level, the pleasure in getting about on two wheels and under your own steam is tremendous. It is an enthusiasm which was given formal recognition when the new Velodrome was located in Manchester - providing a splendid opportunity to nurture local talent, perhaps a future Olympic champion.

The magnificently varied landscape of Lancashire provides outstanding cycling opportunities, so I've found it surprising that the potential for riding its by-ways and bridleways has been largely overlooked. It is an omission which this book should help to redress. Try these routes and share my surprise and delight in the county's diversity - especially appreciated when I return from a long and gruelling continental racing season.

Although few share my good fortune in earning a living from cycling, I meet many for whom it provides a way of life - one that appreciates the unsung features of Britain. These are the qualities that are often found in the villages of deep Lancashire, such as Chipping and Slaidburn, where cyclists gather in the cafés, welcoming young and old to a shared enthusiasm.

I have always been passionate in promoting cycling as beneficial both to an individual's and to society's health. As we travel towards the millennium, surely there is no better way to go than by bike! See you there.

Chris Boardman, MBE

Preface

'Been far?' came the cheerful enquiry from the Vicar of Worsthorne and Cliviger, as he strolled with his wife, exercising their dog along the delightful bridleway that runs due east from their fine village church, straight over the hills to Yorkshire.

'Oh, no, just over the moors and villages and down to the town,' I waved vaguely eastwards like a TV weather forecaster. My reticence was well founded for it transpired that the Reverend Laycock, having recently purchased a bike, had completed a charity ride from Arnside to Worsthorne – a route inevitably hilly or long, and most likely both!

What had earlier been a miserably wet day was now transforming into a stunning sunset. We paused to drink in the atmosphere as the sun slipped below the horizon, the late summer sky ablaze with a glorious, flaming sheet of red. Gazing over the rough, gritstone wall, past the villagers' allotments and across the valley, we could see the darkly brooding mass of Pendle, its ridge and 1800ft summit splendidly silhouetted against the dancing sky, now developing into spectral bands. It was not until the drive back through Burnley that the flames were extinguished, its tracers turned to grey as the night took charge.

Is this a quintessential Lancashire by-way biking experience? It certainly contains some of the elements that contribute to its unique appeal. Since the boundary changes of 1974, the county is no longer overwhelmed by the great conurbations of Manchester and Liverpool, and now presents a special 'upland English' character - part urban (like Burnley), part rural (Worsthrone), part ancient (bridleway to Widdop). The wild, grouse moorland is both remote and reachable in a half-hour's (uphill!) ride from a great northern town born of the desperate times when it was in the van of the Industrial Revolution.

To-day's Lancashire has a quite different aspect – surprisingly, still largely a secret beyond its boundaries – one that I, despite previous forays on the rock and fell, had almost overlooked, until I discovered a view from the saddle, one that I hope others can also find.

Although travelling but a few hundred miles on Lancashire by-ways, it has been an enlightening experience and perhaps I have indeed 'been far'.

Henry Tindell

Acknowledgements

I should like to thank all of the people I've met on my travels around the county and in the preparation of this book – many of whom have unwittingly helped to make this such an enjoyable experience. Particular thanks to Rev. L. Laycock and not forgetting Martin, bacon butty maker extraordinaire!

I am grateful to Gerald Duckworth & Co Ltd for permission to reproduce extracts from 'Roystone Grange:Wall to Wall History', by Richard Hodges.

Thanks also to the long-suffering Sigma Press team for somehow making a presentable output from such a shambolic input, as I'm surely about as well-organised as a teenager's bedroom! And finally, thanks to my family who have suffered but happily survived – even doing some route-testing – in the cause of the 'three Rs' (reading, riding and writing!).

Dedication

To S, R and A.

Contents

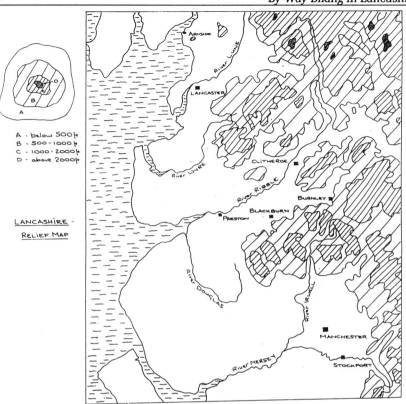

A - below 500ft
B - 500-1000ft
C - 1000-2000ft
D - above 2000ft

LANCASHIRE -
RELIEF MAP

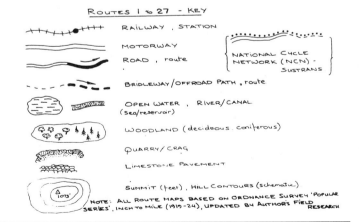

ROUTES 1 to 27 - KEY

RAILWAY , STATION

MOTORWAY

ROAD , route

NATIONAL CYCLE
NETWORK (NCN) -
SUSTRANS

BRIDLEWAY/OFFROAD PATH , route

OPEN WATER , RIVER/CANAL
(sea/reservoir)

WOODLAND (deciduous, coniferous)

QUARRY/CRAG

LIMESTONE PAVEMENT

SUMMIT (feet) , HILL CONTOURS (schematic)

NOTE: ALL ROUTE MAPS BASED ON ORDNANCE SURVEY 'POPULAR
SERIES', INCH TO MILE (1919-24), UPDATED BY AUTHOR'S FIELD
RESEARCH

Lancashire: Relief Map and Routes Key

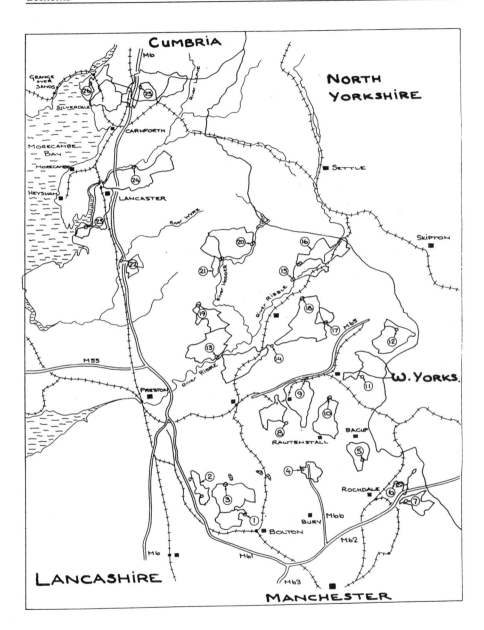

Locations of Routes

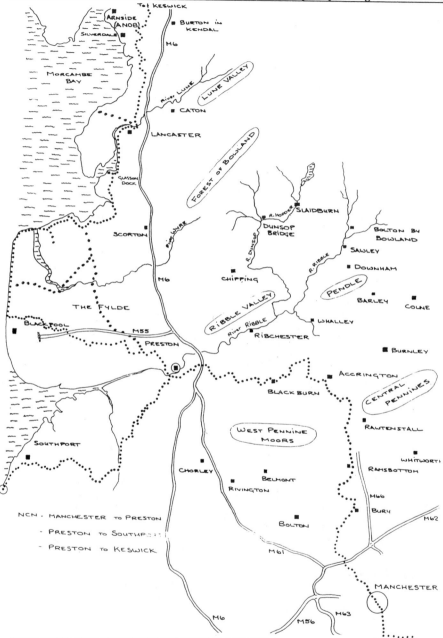

The SUSTRANS National Cycle Network in Lancashire

Lancashire and its By-Ways

'... a terrible heap of houses ... hundreds of high chimneys belching forth like fiery dragons ... over 100,000 men, women and children ... sweating in the vast, hot, stuffy mills and sweltering forges ... growing up stunted, breeding thoughtlessly, dying prematurely ... nor dreaming of ought better than this shrieking, steaming sphere of slime and sorrow.' a (rather melodramatic!) contemporary view of Bolton in the 1890s.

A county with two designated Areas of Outstanding Natural Beauty; the most popular seaside resort and some of the finest coastline and wetlands in the country; surrounded by three National Parks; with outstanding motorway access, and its most remote region within an hour's drive for five-million people – yet this unique resource seems scarcely acknowledged beyond its borders!

Whilst its own country-lovers are well aware of its attractions, to 'outsiders' Lancashire is still tarnished with the cliché of a grimy northern wasteland, redolent of the worst excesses of the Industrial Revolution. Today's reality is soon evident when exploring at first-hand its countryside, villages, towns and cities – and how better than by bike?

The surrounding National Parks – Lake District, Peak District and Yorkshire Dales, have undoubtedly overshadowed Lancashire and its Pennine moors. Since the 1974 boundary changes, however, upland Lancashire has become an essentially rural county, albeit punctuated with some grand Pennine towns. Now relieved of the great sprawling cities of Liverpool, Salford and Manchester, it packs some pleasant surprises.

In the industrial south, places which were once seen (even by Wainwright) only as grimy mill towns teeming with masses of factory workers - such as Bolton, Burnley and Blackburn - are now transforming into centres from which the countryside can be enjoyed, on land or water. The region's saving grace, even in those darkest Victorian hours, has been the towns' allegiance to the moors. The upland south-western region is essentially an extension to the Dark Peak, but lies only minutes from the towns north of Manchester, like Bolton and Bury. These are the West Pennine Moors – for our purposes taking in the hills from the Lancashire plain in the west, to Bury in the east.

The south-eastern upland region has been dubbed the Central Pennines, formed by the gritstone-dominated moorland as far north as Pendle and the Ribble Valley. An area with much in common with the West Pennine Moors, but with its own character; hills that are higher, valleys steeper – this is Lancashire's share of the great Pennine spine of northern England, rising in the Peak and extending to the Cheviots.

The Ribble Valley is our next region, and of an entirely different nature; from its fertile plains it gradually meanders into the foothills of the Pennines. Here, the monasteries of Whalley and Sawley were founded in the 13th century to provide a spiritual (and agricultural!) power-base from which the Church could control the less hospitable uplands.

Although part of the Forest of Bowland AONB, Pendle is displaced south of the Ribble. A self-contained and massive hill, it provides a magnificent area for riding, both around its flanks and into its delightful villages, like Downham, Barley and Sabden.

Beyond the Ribble, the huge upland area of the Forest of Bowland dominates – a formidable mass that bars our way north between the M6 and the Pennines. The villages of Chipping, Dunsop Bridge and Slaidburn provide our bases for the most arduous and remote routes in the county, amidst a landscape that wouldn't be out of place in the Highlands.

Bowland's progress north is interrupted by the Lune Valley, another rich, lowland region, with the City of Lancaster at its head. Its beauty has long been recognised, although often overlooked by modern travellers dashing north. Lancaster is greatly enhanced by the city's enlightened provision of the best cycleways in the county (if not the country – imagine similar routes through London, along the Victoria embankment!), providing miles of exquisite off-road riding along the banks of the Lune – stretching from Glasson Dock at the estuary, to the Crook O' Lune beauty spot, far inland.

Our journey is finally curtailed at the Arnside and Silverdale AONB, although we also travel west across the M6 and into the Farleton Crag region, surprisingly not included in the AONB despite its distinctive and now-protected 'limestone pavements'. A tiny gem of an area!

These first twenty-six routes are circular, and in almost all cases start from a car park or picnic site, with easy road access from Lancashire's extensive motorway and trunk road network – apart from the Bowland routes. In many instances these routes can be readily accessed by rail, which is to be encouraged – although I admit to failing this practise, despite good intentions, so far.

The final route is undoubtedly the pièce de résistance: an eighty-six mile, two-day, linear route along the entire length of the county. From just north of the boundary at Arnside, it makes fleeting contact with the sea and continues along Route 26 (Silverdale) before tackling one of England's finest off-road tracks, over the Bowland fells to Slaidburn. Accommodation is available at the youth hostel or the Hark to Bounty inn. The final day takes in plenty of road hills en route to the Anglian village of Downham, and some of the best bridleways of the Pendle and Whalley routes. Despite a relatively short recourse to A-roads, we are soon back to quiet lanes and the delights of the West Pennine Moors once again, at Rivington. The concluding section follows the return leg of our first route, to a fitting finale at the historic setting of Smithill's Hall. Just a couple of miles further is Bolton, with its excellent road and rail access.

Whilst each route is described in detail (where the devil is!), a 'summary page' is provided for easier use 'in-the-field'. Applying the old maxim 'if all else fails, read the instructions' may well be sufficient, but the descriptions should, I hope, be of use in gauging the terrain, and especially in route-finding. And there is often just a whisker (as in battle) between a glorious and exhilarating outing and a desperate and miserable struggle – often hinging on one's mental approach, and perhaps the weather! Whilst a fair degree of fitness and application is necessary to complete the full itinerary, this is by no means beyond the ability of anyone keen enough. At the other end of the scale, there are several routes that are suitable (with proper care) for family outings and/or on 'any old bike', to which I can testify!

One last thing – do be careful to protect the interests of others by a rigorous respect for the countryside and its inhabitants. Fitting a bell is one of the few accessories that I would strongly advocate – for unwittingly surprising others from behind is a clear danger, even for the most careful rider. We pass through some wonderful countryside, but nowhere should we leave but the slightest of traces – contrast the ghastly damage done by four-wheel-drive vehicles and the like near Croasedale Fell. Adopting an 'enlightened self-interest' attitude ensures that soft ground is easily circumvented, and on steep hills a short carry is often the most efficient way.

The game, as Sherlock Holmes would say, is afoot!

Getting Ready

'Turn, turn my wheel! Turn round and round, without a pause, without a sound.' Longfellow

Planning

Rating

This is an entirely subjective 'quality' value akin to that used in climbing guides – where there is often a surprising consensus of opinion about what constitutes a 'three-star' route. We shall see!

> zero stars - unclassified, see text
> * - Good route
> ** - Excellent route
> *** - Outstanding route

Grading

A measure of difficulty, based on a mixture of off-road terrain and length. It also includes cross-country route-finding difficulties, so a route may be rated 'Difficult' in either or both of these respects. The 'severe' category is reserved for routes requiring some experience and/or stamina to enjoyably complete. These gradings will often be subject to prevailing weather conditions.

Gradient

Simply a measure of the steepness of the off-road sections, taking little or no account of on-road hills. These can normally be walked with relative ease – on really steep ('A') or slippery off-road, this may not be the case! Most of the routes, however, fall into the medium ('B') category, with the easy ('C') rating reserved for those that really are pretty flat off-road, and thus easily tackled by inexperienced riders.

Rights of Way

The key to the best riding in Lancashire is its bridleways and quiet country lanes. But it is vital to have an understanding of our Rights of Way, in order to enjoy this freedom, without fear of trespass or upsetting others. Simply put, all public ways of a higher status than footpaths are legitimate places to ride. Footpaths are definitely not for riding on! Bridleways, BOATs (By-ways Open to All Traffic), RUPPs (Roads Used as Public Paths), permissive paths, and all roads open to the public are a Right of Way for cyclists (apart from specific exclusions such as motorways or restricted places).

It is essential, however, that bridleways (where the vast majority of our off-road riding is done) are treated with proper respect, remembering that priority is firstly to those on foot, then horseback, both taking precedence over cyclists. Always observe utmost care on such tracks for this is a right that, through misuse, could be lost. Permissive paths (bridleway status) normally provide access, but this is at the ultimate discretion of the landowner – so the same, scrupulously careful, approach is vital. Rights of Way can, and do, change but only through the proper procedure, which safeguards legitimate users from the whim of a landowner who wants to unilaterally downgrade an established bridleway to a footpath – isolated cases of which I have encountered. On the other hand, there are cases where paths have been legally up- (or down-) graded, although in practice this always takes a long time. Therefore, even the latest OS map is only a guide to Rights of Way. On a contentious path the current status must be checked with the local authority or Rights of Way official. Contact numbers are provided in the Useful Information section.

Preparation

Selecting and preparing a machine is a subject best pursued elsewhere. For the inexperienced, probably the first place to seek advice is the local, friendly bike shop that not only sells, but services (and preferably rides!) its bikes; or an organisation with local members, such as the CTC or YHA (see Useful Information). Although a handful of these routes can be covered with 'any old bike', naturally a 'mountain bike' is preferable for the remainder, which is little problem as they have now become so popular for general use. A suitable mount should feature a good selection of low gears; simple, sturdy construction; big tyres; and (often overlooked as an important feature) relatively low weight. If choosing a bike, it is well worth trying to carry it uphill to compare this – it may be appreciated later on!

Running a bike is just simple common sense, ensuring that all moving parts are liberally oiled – modern (i.e. expensive!) lubricants now enabling one to achieve this without turning self and stead into the proverbial oily rag. Perhaps the most important riding tip is to avoid, like the plague, transferring significant portions of the landscape onto the 'drive' – unless one is near base and intends to dispose of the machine forthwith! By avoiding any unnecessary contamination one preserves countryside, self and bike; thus retaining a highly efficient and elegant machine – rather than an awful, grinding wreck (to say nothing of the bike!).

Preparing self is a matter for the individual, but I have found that riding is one of the best (i.e. least painful) methods of getting fit, or at least becoming slightly less unfit! When legs weary of pedalling uphill, a spell pushing relieves tired muscles, and the ascent is (eventually!) inevitably followed by downhill. The capacity to vary pace to suit conditions means that, with a little practice, one can ride (between refreshment stops!) all day long, in the manner of a long walk, but without the constant standing up! Like any physical activity, it is a matter of working up to one's chosen level – but beware, it can become highly addictive, a habit that can last a lifetime.

The layout and summaries of the routes should provide a guide against which to pit one's abilities. Although the 'best' routes are not necessarily the 'hardest' (or vice-versa), increasing capabilities do expand one's choice. Safety, on and off-road, must always be borne in mind, remembering one's vulnerability – against other road users and against nature in the hills. Obviously, proper precautions like basic first aid practice and wearing the appropriate gear is important, but the right mental approach is perhaps the best safeguard to maintaining a safe balance along the knife-edge of life, in by-way biking as much as in anything else worth the candle.

A By-Way Biking Code

✦ Do **not** ride on footpaths.

✦ Ride carefully off-road and on. Think about and practice safety, always.

✦ Apply all the normal, common sense Country Code rules, leaving it as found.

✦ Be careful not to endanger others – on bridleways always give way to those on foot or horseback.

✦ Give proper warning of approach from behind (a bell is recommended), allowing plenty of time.

✦ Respect the rights and needs of others in the countryside, especially those whose livelihood depends directly upon it.

✦ Don't endanger self, others, or our future Right of Way.

✦ Prepare appropriately, apply mountain safety principles as needed, and keep to a decent safety margin.

✦ Have fun – I certainly did!

Useful Information

Tourist Information Centres (TICs)

Accrington: Town Hall, Blackburn Rd; tel. 01254 872595
Burnley: The Bus Station; tel. 01282 423125
Charnock Richard: M6 Services, Chorley; tel. 01257 793773
Clitheroe: 12-14, Market Place; tel. 01200 44226
Lancaster: 29, Castle Hill; tel. 01254 841656
Morecambe: Station Bldg., Central Promenade; tel. 01524 582808
Nelson: The Bus Station, Broadway; tel. 01282 698533
Preston: The Bus Station; tel. 01772 556618
Rossendale: Kay St., Rawtenstall; tel. 01706 213677

Country Parks

Beacon Fell Country Park, Bowland; tel. 01995 640557

Wycoller Country Park, Trawden Rd, Wycoller, Colne.

Organisations

CTC (Cyclists' Touring Club), Cotterel Ho., 69, Meadrow, Godolming, Surrey, GU7 3HS

BCF (British Cycling Federation), National Cycling Centre, Stuart St., Manchester, M11 4DQ

VCC (Veteran Cycling Club), c/o Geoff Paine, 31, Yorke Rd, Croxley Green, Rickmansworth, Herts. WD3 3DW

South Pennines Packhorse Trails Trust, The Barn, Makinholes, Todmorden, OL14 6HR.

Youth Hostels Association (YHA)

Arnside, tel. 01524 761781

Slaidburn, tel. 01200 446656

Earby (nr. Colne), tel. 01282 842349

Manchester (centre), tel. 0161 839 9960

Accommodation, refreshments and repairs

Accommodation is possibly most easily sourced through the excellent booking service at the TICs. For the last route, there is accommodation at the seaside town of Arnside, with the YHA being a particularly appropriate place to stay. Slaidburn also boasts the King's House YHA and Hark to Bounty inn. At the finish, Bolton has all the facilities one would expect from a major town, and the Manchester YHA is easily reached by train.

The most popular source of refreshments is the country (or town) pub, at least one of which is passed on each route (with the sole exception of Grizedale, although Scorton has an alternative). A particular delight to the discerning cyclist is the tea shop. Unfortunately, there is not one available on all routes, although particularly fine examples can be found on the Chipping, Barley, Crook O' Lune and Silverdale rides, plus many others (see *Tea Shop Walks in Lancashire* in the Bibliography).

Bike shops are available in many of the towns, some particularly familiar with their local off-road riding. Some also hire, including:

✦ D. Tours, Horwich; tel. 01204 699460

✦ Pedal Power, Clitheroe; tel. 01200 422066

✦ Cycle 2000, Lancaster; tel. 01524 381414

Abbreviations used in the summaries:

BW – bridleway; FP – footpath; Resr. – reservoir; T-jn – T-junction;
SP – signpost; TR - turn right; TL - turn left; SO - straight on; Resr. - reservoir

Units

⊕ height in feet
⊕ distance in miles
⊕ short distances in metres (assume 1 metre = 1 yard)
⊕ refreshment in pints!

These units may not make an EC commissar beam with joy, but are the ones most in sympathy with the routes – who wants to gain height at a miserly rate measured in metres? That may be fine for the Alps, but let's keep our one, two and three-thousand footer English hills for as long as possible!

Rights of Way Contacts

Hyndburn District Council – tel. 01254 388111
Lancashire Ranger's Office – tel. 01772 264709
Pendle Borough Council – tel. 01282 661661
Ribble Valley Borough Council – tel. 01200 425111
Forest of Bowland County Council – tel. 01772 264140

Bibliography

Tea Shop Walks in Lancashire, Clive Price, Sigma Press, 1997.

West Pennine Walks, Mike Cresswell, Sigma Press, 1988.

Walks on the West Pennine Moors, Gladys Sellars, Cicerone Press, 1978.

The Making of the Central Pennines, John Porter, Moorland Press, 1980.

Historic Walks in the Ribble Valley, John Dixon, Dalesman Press, 1987.

Walks in the Arnside and Silverdale AONB, R.Brian Evans, Cicerone Press, 1986.

Bowland and Pendle, WR Mitchell, Smith Settle, 1993.

Walks in Lancashire Witch Country, Jack Keighley, Cicerone Press, 1992.

Walking the Peak and Pennines, Mike Harding, Michael Joseph, 1992.

Mountain Bike Lancashire & South Pennines, Richard Peace, Excellent Books, 1996.

Lancashire Countrygoer, Jessica Lofthouse, Hale, 1974.

The Treasures of Lancashire, North West Civic Trust, 1989.

A History of Lancashire, J.J. Bagley, Phillimore, 1970.

The Village Atlas, 1840 – 1912, The Alderman Press, 1989.

The West Pennine Moors

Winter Hill dominates the western fringe of this conservation area, a focus for walking, fell running, rock-climbing, sailing, fishing, birdwatching, and much more. At 1501ft, and with subsidiary tops like the 1192ft Rivington Pike, it has a long history. Evidence of settlements around the Rivington and Anglezarke moors dates back at least to the Bronze Age, but unfortunately little obvious remains for the casual visitor to see. Despite this, while walking on Noon Hill or through Lead Mines Clough it needs little imagination to perceive the aura of prehistory. As the New Stone Age was characterised by periods of considerably higher temperatures than today, habitation in upland areas like Winter Hill was likely to be perfectly viable. A foretaste of our presently much-vaunted global warming? The Vikings certainly settled around the western slopes of these hills, where the Rivington Great Barns now stand, striking links with the past and variously dated between Saxon and medieval times.

Beyond these villages and hamlets, the towns of Horwich, Bolton and Bury were drawn into the explosive growth of the 18th and 19th centuries, mirrored in the Central Pennines. The demands for labour to feed the burgeoning textile industries of Bolton and Bury saw their populations expand ten-fold in the 19th century. Key inventions, like the 'Mule' of Bolton's Samuel Crompton, and Kay's 'Flying Shuttle', made these Lancashire towns wealthy – witness their magnificent stone civic centres that date from this period. However, records show that lamentably little was spent on the more mundane public health needs of the masses of millworkers. The strains of this growth were not really relieved until the similarly dramatic decline in manufacturing which has accelerated since the 1950s, creating different problems, but also the chance to revalue their greatest asset – the moors.

Late in Victoria's reign, the 'model village' of Barrow Bridge (see Route 1) was developed – for workers needed accommodation within easy walking distance of the mills. We find a paternal employer providing for their needs, with his bakery producing 200 loaves a day for the millworkers of the 1890s. At the same time, a mile downstream at Smithills Hall (end of Route 27), the owner of the nearby bleach works, one Colonel Henry Richard Ainsworth, precipitated what was to become the first Mass Trespass. The working folk of Bolton gathered, some 10 000-strong, to walk over forbidden ground across Smithills Moor. The Colonel had decreed that his estate (extending to Winter Hill summit) should be kept as an enclosed grouse moor. So the local people, galvanised by the Bolton Socialist Party, organised a series of audacious marches from Halliwell, north Bolton, past Smithills Hall and up Coal Pit Road to the summit of Winter Hill – to the chagrin of the Colonel, and his burly band of gamekeepers. This remarkable event, pre-dating the famous Kinder Mass Trespass of 1932 by 35 years, was followed by the Colonel (being a JP) exacting his revenge in a crippling court case against the marchers' leaders. By the 1950s, however, the estate had passed to Bolton Council and the moors were opened to access; but it wasn't until the centenary in 1996 that the actual path was re-established as a Right of Way, and marked by the fine, carved gritstone commemorative stone seen on Route 3.

In the last century, half of Rivington was submerged in the reservoirs created to satisfy Liverpool's ever-increasing demand for water – but what remains is actually enhanced. Large tracts of the country leading up to the Pike were purchased in 1900 by William Lever – later Lord Leverhulme, founder of the Lever Bros. empire. His birthplace in Wood Street, central Bolton, could be passed on the way from the railway station to our first route. It was Leverhulme's generosity that saw this estate transformed into a park and Chinese Gardens. He even established a zoo and the ultimate rich man's folly – a replica of the long-vanished, ruined Liverpool Castle, which we visit on Route 2.

Further east, we begin the last of this series near Holcombe and the Peel Tower, finding hilly and colourful countryside around Ramsbottom. Happily, this is still accessible despite the passage of the M66, over which we pass easily on a bridleway. These towns and villages may be off the tourist trail, but are well worth visiting – and the floodlit view of the tower (built by residents' subscription in honour of local hero, Robert Peel, Prime Minister) will surely strike the memory as one flees along a dark M66.

Altogether a good introduction to the hills of south Lancashire – combining excellent accessibility and routes with a fair range of difficulty around fine country. Expansive views and some prime refreshment opportunities provide a useful precursor to the more (or less!) demanding routes further north and west.

Route 1 – Barrow Bridge

Distance: 15 miles
Off-road: 30%
Height Gain: 1050ft
Time: 2 – 3 hours
Start/Finish: Car park, Barrow Bridge, N. Bolton. GR 687 117
Maps: OS Landranger 109, Explorer 19
Rating: *
Grading: Moderate
Gradient: B

'Lancashire is now so largely devoted to manufacture and trade that many scarcely think of it as a county full of historic interest.' Prof. Ernest Axon, 1892

Route Summary

A civilised introduction to the beginning of the West Pennine Moors, with easy access from central Bolton – either direct by road, or via Bolton railway

Barrow Bridge

station, a couple of miles from the start. Route finding is not too difficult, although attention to detail will ensure a safe ride on the bridleways across the golf courses – rather than a dangerous one across the greens! Very pleasant paths provide fine panoramas to the south of Winter Hill, that first great bastion of open moorland north of Manchester.

Off-road, the bridleways are neither long nor arduous, and are endowed with surfaces little affected by weather or season. Apparently a 'soft touch' for the mountain-biker, nevertheless the ride uphill from Horwich to Smithills Hall shouldn't be too readily discounted!

Recommended as a fairly short, interesting route with plenty of local colour, fine views and enjoyable off-road riding, where, not for the last time, a little effort is handsomely rewarded.

Route Description

a) – b)

The excellent car park is readily found near the end of Barrow Bridge's sole road. Turn left out of the car park and past the row of magnificent old mill cottages, alongside the stream which runs deeply between the sturdy gritstone walls.

Immediately before the lane swings sharply right in the direction of Winter Hill, we continue straight on along the bridleway, taking the left fork and rising uphill. An excellent stony track, it nevertheless provides a stout test of one's resolve to ride all the way! A short push leads to a more amenable gradient and a cobbled track between drystone wall and hedge – quintessentially Lancashire by-way biking! Following the obvious track, we crest the rise and cross the golf course, now with views right towards Winter Hill (its ubiquitous relay mast identifying the summit) and left to Bolton and Horwich. The cinder track becomes cobbled again, and leads delightfully down to meet the road.

Turn left along Walker Fold Rd and shortly down to the crossroads at Bob's Smithy pub. Go across the B6226 Bolton-Horwich road, heading straight on, and still downhill on Old Kiln Lane. Continue on a pleasant section through the fine avenue of tall trees to the crossing of the dual carriageway (take care).

b) – c)

Continue straight on over this main Bolton Rd, continuing along Old Kiln Lane. Past the white cottages on the left, we turn right up Markland Hill. Go past Markland High School and Lingmell Close and then downhill through this pleasant, leafy suburb, around some sweeping bends and past the Victoria Inn, to the junction at the bottom.

Turn left and along the major road for half a mile, then turn right into Overdale Drive (signposted – 'Overdale Crematorium' and 'Public footpath,

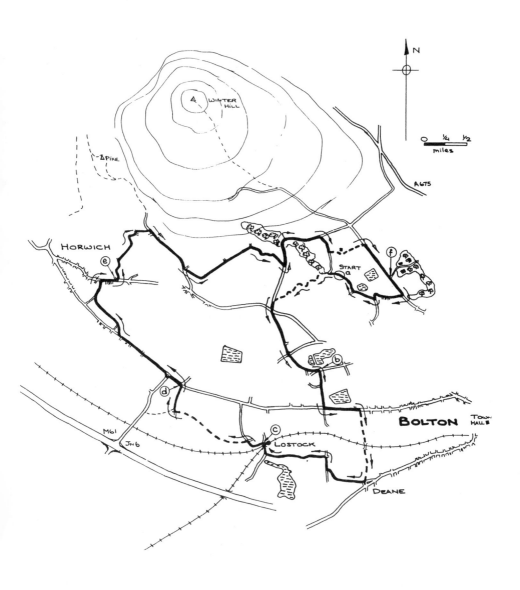

Route 1: Barrow Bridge

(Deane,1'). Continue until the track becomes unmetalled, but still with a good all-weather surface. Ignoring the left for the crematorium, we continue straight on downhill, past the flower nursery to the bottom (slightly muddy here), then uphill on a rideable track. Shortly we reach the junction with the road at Deane, with the Stag's Head on the left.

Turn right and immediately go past the King's Head on the minor road to a T-junction in 100 metres. Turn right, past Deane Golf Club clubhouse on Lismore Rd. Past the Beaumont Arms and downhill as we parallel the main road on the left. Continue down, to take the first left to the traffic lights with the main road (just after Greenham Close and the school). Turn right at the lights and go along the A58 for 100 metres to the next lights, where we turn left, along Lostock Rd West (signposted – 'Lostock'). Back to the countryside with agricultural views to our left. Pleasant riding downhill to the T-junction where we turn right. After 100 metres, turn left over the railway bridge and stream into Regent Rd (Lostock Station is just beyond).

c) – d)

Follow Regent Rd as it runs alongside the railway track, until it swings right. Opposite Sandfield Drive and the postbox we turn left down an unmarked gravel track – between waney-lap fences. The track is 2 metres wide but easily missed. Go past the 'no-tipping' sign and out across the golf course – still on an excellent, well-surfaced track – I must admit it gives me a small frisson of pleasure to legally ride through the middle of such hallowed grounds! Fine views again, towards Winter Hill on the right. Continue straight on, ignoring a left to the clubhouse, until the track becomes partly concrete, but still most pleasant riding. Across the cattle grid and, as the Lostock Hall Farm is approached, Rivington Pike is revealed far away on the right. At the wide metal gate of the farm we turn right – initially on a metalled track, then a more broken surface leading to Oxhey Lane. This heads up to a T-junction with the Horwich road.

d) – e)

Turn left and shortly reach a vast roundabout. Continue straight on to Horwich, thankfully now on a cycle lane. Immediately after the Towel Mill-Shop and Chorley New Rd Primary School on the left, we turn right up Victoria Rd and past Bolton College – Horwich campus. On past St. John's Methodist church until Ramsbottom Rd joins from the left. Continue straight on to the T-junction at the end of Victoria Rd, where we turn right. On past the police station, Black Bull, parish school, fine church and the Brown Cow, after which we turn left along Mill Lane – its name mounted high on the wall end.

e) – f)

Mill Lane leads into Foxholes Rd and back out to the country, keeping right at the fork, as we climb steeply up the charming lane. On past Marklands

House and Stoneycroft Hall, with the final rise to the T-junction demanding a fair effort!

Turn right at this junction, and the road now follows the contours of Winter Hill, revealing fine views west across the Lancashire and Cheshire plain, with the new Bolton Wanderers stadium prominent near the Horwich roundabout passed earlier.

Just as the road begins to descend, turn left sharply then bear immediately right and along Matchmoor Lane, (ignoring the track running directly up Winter Hill). Continue along the exposed gritstone-walled lane, where the combination of a steady rise, wind and the previous climb from Horwich may be found to take their toll! Eventually past the sign proclaiming 'Welcome to Smithills Hall and Park' as the road declines towards the T-junction. Turn left and press on over the undulating and twisting road, and past Colliers Row Farm (the bridleway on Route 2 goes left from here). Another 150 metres and at the next farmhouse we turn right down Longshaw Ford Rd. Now it's nicely downhill to the broad bridleway entrance marked by a good, wooden 'Right of Way' signpost, where we turn left. Follow the obvious track between walls and hedges as it passes the cottages and bends right and left, before running delightfully down to meet Smithills Dean Rd. Turn right here, continuing (thankfully!) downhill for 200 metres to Smithills Hall entrance on the left.

f) – a)

Continue straight on past Smithills Hall to the bottom of the hill and then turn right into Smithills Croft Rd, which is followed beyond the sharp bend to the large chimney and the T-junction at Moss Lane/ Barrow Bridge Rd. Turn right along Barrow Bridge Rd, past the rolling fields of the park and into the narrow lane of Barrow Bridge. Past the bus turning-space, the start is reached just beyond the row of cottages – those on the right a riot of colour with their gardens tumbling down to the stream. A long way, surely, from those dark, satanic mills.

Summary

a) – b)
TL out of car park
SO into BW, fork L (uphill), and across golf course
TL at rd
SO over crossroads at Bob's Smithy – along Old Kiln Lane

b) – c)
SO over Bolton Rd dual carriageway
TR up Markland Hill, past Victoria Inn
TL at T-jn, SO for ½ ml
TR into Overdale Drive (SP – FP Deane, 1)
SO along BW
TR on rd, past Kings Head to T-jn
TR along Lismore Rd
TL to traffic lights at A58
TR along A58 for 100m to traffic lights
TL along Lostock Rd West to T-jn
TR and in 100m over bridge

c) – d)
TL into Regent Rd
TL into BW (unmarked) opposite Sandfield Dr.
SO along BW to Lostock Hall Fm., across golf course
TR at fm, cont. SO along Oxhey Lane to T-jn.

d) – e)
TL along Horwich Rd to roundabout
SO towards Horwich for ½ml
TR up Victoria Rd, bear R to T-jn.
TR past pubs, church & Brown Cow and immed. -

e) – f)
TL into Mill Lane, leading to Foxholes Rd
R at fork & steep uphill to T-jn
TR until rd begins to descend
TL (sharp) & immed. TR into Matchmoor Lane, to T-jn.
TL and past Colliers Fm, & in 150m -
TR into Longshaw Ford Rd
TL into BW (SP OK) SO to Smithills Dean Rd

f) – a)
TR to bottom of hill (SO past Smithills Hall)
TR into Smithills Croft Rd to T-jn
TR into Barrow Bridge Rd, SO for ¾ml
TL into car park.

Route 2 – Rivington

Distance: 12 miles

Off-road: 72%

Height Gain: 600ft

Time: $2\frac{1}{2}$ – $3\frac{1}{2}$ hours

Start/Finish: Great Barn (Info Centre & car park), Rivington, nr. Horwich. GR 628 138

Maps: O.S. Landranger 109, Explorer 19 West Pennine Moors

Rating: ***

Grading: Moderate

Gradient: B

'When Rivington puts on her hood
She fears a rainy day
But when she doffs it you will find
The rain is o'er, and still the wind
And Phoebus shines away!'

Traditional weather rhyme

Route Summary

I've chosen this as my only short and not-too-serious three-star route. Whether I was just lucky in having a perfect summer's evening and little pressure of time and this influenced me too much, I don't know, but I found this route pure delight. Maybe others will disagree, but my memories are set!

The bridleways are well marked, an example to all others – unfortunately, not all landowners encountered on later travels live up to this standard. Whilst the tracks were dry and perfect for riding in summer, there are some places that could be less amenable in the winter. A sensible approach, however, should enable a good ride to be made under less favourable conditions – many alternatives exist, some of which are described in the Info Centre at the Great Barn. The only possible drawback that this wonderful area can possibly have is its popularity – at its best early or late in the day (or year!), and easy access makes it a great evening's outing. A fascinating history surrounds the area, outlined in the description of the West Pennine Moors.

Route Description

a) – b)

The Great Barn makes an ideal starting point unless you arrive, as I did, for a summer evening's ride – for the barrier to the car park closes at 6.30pm! Fortunately, there is an excellent alternative just across the road on the track to the Great Hall, another building of great historical and immediate interest, as it also provides refreshments!

From the Great Barn car park, continue on the good, unmetalled path heading straight for the reservoir. Bear right, following the blue arrow, then turn left after 20 metres and straight on down the short slope to reach a well-made wooden fence – beyond which lie the trees fringing the reservoir, some 50 metres ahead. At the fence we turn left, following the delightful, unsurfaced track down a dip and over a wooden bridge. Follow the track, keeping close to the fence, with the reservoir never far away to our right, until it emerges from the wood, continuing straight on as another track joins from the left. This affords a glimpse of the Pigeon Tower and Rivington Pike on the skyline. The track now leads back through glorious riding to the shore, then a gravelled surface where we bear slightly left, and suddenly reach the 'castle'. This extraordinary building is actually an unfinished replica of the ruined Liverpool Castle – the details of which are displayed on an information board. Simply a rich man's folly, and why not?

b) – c)

Exit the castle from the information board, heading down the grand (unsurfaced) avenue, still bridleway, in the direction of the Pike. Straight on, past the car park on the right, to the gate then a T-junction with the road. Turn left along the road and straight on past Knowle House, after which we turn right into a wooded area, along a small track marked with a good bridleway sign. This delightful track runs past hollies, and begins to rise up the wooded slope to meet the broad, open track that crosses in 200 metres. A fine contrast to the previous tracks , this part does tend to hold the odd muddy patch, but these are easily circumvented, a good excuse for a push!

Turn left on to the broad track, which is enclosed by a magnificent avenue of trees. As it declines it provides sublime riding with occasional glimpses of the reservoir on the left. Continue straight on past the house on the right. Just after the cottage on the left, at the junction of tracks, turn right – the track now rising a little. Continue straight on past the next junction, now with views up the hillside on the right to the Pigeon Tower which we meet on Route 3. Through another wooded area as the track makes a rightward curve to take the right fork, then straight on, following the bridleway arrow. Now a broad track, it runs between low fences and we keep straight on, running hard to the left of a drystone wall enclosing woodland. In 50 metres it finally meets a main track at a T-junction. Turn right and go along

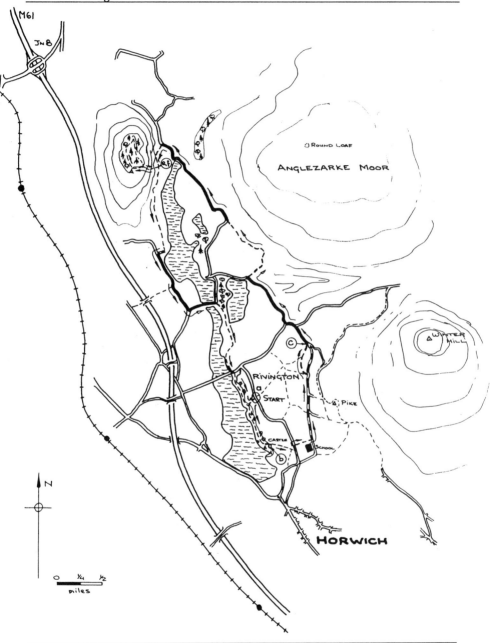

Route 2: Rivington

the track bounded by a fence and a drystone wall, shortly arriving at a gate with the road just beyond. Across the road is the car park, conveniently sited for a quick visit to the Pigeon Tower and the Pike.

c) – d)

Turn left and go along the pleasant road towards Rivington, going straight on as the road from Belmont feeds in from the right, following the cycleway sign. Downhill for another 200 metres to a T-junction, where we turn right following the sign 'Anglezarke 1¾, Heapy 4¼'. There are magnificent views – behind is Winter Hill, all around are rolling fields enclosed by gritstone walls, and ahead lies Anglezarke reservoir. Continue straight on downhill past the farm with '1670' carved in the stone door lintel. In no time the downhill brings us to the bridge across the neck of the reservoir, and we turn right immediately after the bridge, following the well-signed bridle-way through the gate. In the few minutes I paused here on a balmy sum-mer's evening, it was gratifying to see more riders (bikes and horses) than cars – a delightful spot. The fine track, shaded by trees, runs between stone walls alongside the stream, initially flat. Crossing the stream by the small bridge, we continue along the obvious track and past the information board about Lead Mines Clough. At the fork we turn left and go over the stone bridge, following the white arrow up a track that soon demands a push. A superb track, it shortly leads to a gate with a massive chain, through which we easily pass. Go straight on, following the white arrow up the hill and keeping hard to the left of the wire fence. Over the top of the hill and the ex-cellent track invites more pedalling along the edge of the field. The views are again panoramic – back to Winter Hill and the reservoirs, and across to-wards Horwich. A farm can now be seen about a mile ahead. Continue straight on through the next gate, now along a gravelled track between a ditch and fence. Straight on through another couple of metal gates and then a wooden one, following a white arrow, finally reaching the lane after some pleasant riding over high ground.

d) – e)

Go straight on along the lane (ignoring the road coming in from the left), and down past Manor Farm. Continue downhill, along Moor Lane, with tre-mendous views out across the valley. This becomes Higher House Lane as it finally reaches the bottom and begins to climb past Cliff Farm, with the inscription 'TARM – 1696' above the door – but the romantic ambience of the cottage is somewhat rudely counterbalanced by the adjacent modern bungalow and pile of scrap cars! Immediately opposite the cottage we turn left into a well-signed bridleway (horse's head motif), and up a steadily ris-ing, delightful little track. In summer the hedgerows sport a profusion of wildlife, foxgloves being particularly prominent. The track presents just enough small boulders to make it more profitable to push for a short while, and enjoy this idyllic path. After the steady climb the gradient relents to comfortably rideable going along the dry track, now affording views across to the left of Winter Hill as we approach the turn off to Healy Nab.

e) – f)

Along this level part we reach a signpost with the legend 'Public Bridleway, Concessionary'. This is a small diversion too good to be missed, so we turn right and follow the sign towards the summit, Healy Nab. The good track leads cross-country alongside a wire fence, over the rise and along the flat. Turn left at the junction and follow the white arrows for 50 metres to a gate. Go straight on through this and hard along the left of the wood, following another white sign indicating the concessionary route. Up the rise to the top of Healy Nab – much to my surprise, I arrived here in the late evening to find a troupe of cub-scouts had already occupied the high ground. But the riding is superb, so we push on over the top and follow the narrow track as it leads down over a number of erosion-control boards (care) to a gate. Immediately before the gate make an acute right turn and head back up the hill, still in the thick of the wood. The narrow ribbon of track proves to be just about rideable as it runs through ferns, bearing left to the small outcrop of rocks then left again. Following another white arrow, through a more sandy patch. Then it's a short push, a pedal over the top and down through woods again. Through the glade and bear right, then left after 50 metres to a small gate. Go straight on, still following the concessionary signs out to open ground. Bear right, past the fenced-off old quarry and another white sign leads back to our way up from the original turn off. Now there's a great ride down. This is actually much more simple to follow than it might sound, and only takes a quarter of an hour, but respect the concessionary track and other users – the route is also a favourite with horse riders and walkers.

f) – a)

A right turn returns us to the original route, which is followed delightfully downhill on an excellent track. Over to the left can be seen the quarried faces of Anglezarke, beyond the reservoir. Go straight on, following the bridleway arrows, over the foot-high board as a track joins from the right. In 250 metres the track has descended to the level of the reservoir and we reach Heathfold, then Kay's Farm, leaving the evening sun casting a glorious golden light across the water and on to the rocks. At Kay's Farm turn right along the concrete road to meet the public road at a T-junction – the end of a fine bridleway. Turn left and go past fields of cows and a farm then the occasional cottage – some way to the right the M61 can just about be discerned, but it does not intrude on this fine country lane with its hedgerows of wild flowers. Finally, along to the T-junction where we leave Back Lane and turn left along Knowsley Lane. Across the junction, the Yew Tree stands invitingly. This junction has the name Dill Hall Brow. We follow the signpost to Anglezarke and Belmont, which soon leads us over the reservoir.

At the far side of the reservoir, a bridleway sign indicates a right turn up through the wood and alongside the weir, with the odd patch of mud ,but nothing to spoil the fun. A return to the saddle is soon possible and a last stout effort will see one successfully up the rise and making a right turn at the junction. The excellent track now takes a level way around the embankment on the left, with a drystone wall holding the wood back on the right. The track now descends gently, making for delightful riding all the way to the gate, where we continue straight on. Continue along the metalled lane to reach a T-junction, with the Rivington Village Club on the left and reservoirs in most other directions!

Turn left towards Rivington, but after only 50 metres turn right, following the wooden bridleway signpost, and go past the village school. The school lies somewhat below and to the left of our track. Continue up the sandy track, through the row of posts, and straight on (ignoring the track off to the left). The track levels and even declines as it follows the line of the reservoir, seen behind the trees to the right. A lovely track, it soon brings us back to the outward route, where we turn left back to the Great Barn – anyone for another lap?

Rivington (Anglezarke Reservoir)

Summary

a) – b)
SO from Great Barn car park, towards Resr.
bear R, following BW arrow
TL after 20m
TL at fence, follow track around shoreline
SO at main track to 'castle'

b) – c)
SO from castle, heading for Pike, on BW avenue
TL along rd
TR into small wood (BW, SP)
SO up wood to main track
TL and along main track
TR at BW jn, SO (BW, SPs), bear R, SO to track jn.
TR and along to gate (BW exit) – opposite is car park for Pigeon Tower

c) – d)
TL and downhill on rd
SO
TR at SP 'Anglezarke 1¾, Heapy 4¼'
SO to bottom, over Resr. bridge
TR into BW (SP) immed after bridge
SO to Lead Mines Clough
TL, over bridge and uphill
SO, following white arrows, 1ml to Rd (exit BW)

d) – e)
SO along rd, downhill past Manor Fm
TL into BW (off Higher House Lane), opposite Cliff Fm
SO along BW to top of rise

e) – f)
TR – concessionary BW loop to Healy Nab
Follow marking around the Nab and return to original BW

f) – a)
TR and continue on original BW
SO, downhill to Kay's FM
TR along track to rd, exit BW
TL along lane to T-jn (Back Lane)
TL – opposite is Yew Tree
SO along Knowsley Lane, across Resr.
TR immed. far side Resr. into BW (SP)
SO uphill past weir
TR and along main track to rd
SO at rd to T-jn at Rivington Club and Resr
TL, and in 50m -
TR into BW, past school, thro' posts
SO along shoreline track to meet outward track
TL and back to start.

Route 3 – Belmont

Distance: 14 miles
Off-road: 31%
Height Gain: 1300ft
Time: 2 -3 hours
Start/Finish: Blue Lagoon (car park!), Belmont, (Belmont to Rivington road). GR 667 158
Maps: OS Landranger 109, Explorer 19
Rating: *
Grading: Moderate
Gradient: B

'Will Yo come O' Sunday Mornin'
Fo a walk O'er Winter Hill?
Ten thousand went last Sunday
But there's room for thousands still!'
Allen Clarke, Winter Hill Mass Trespass, 1896

Route Summary

This is essentially a circumnavigation of Winter Hill, a fascinating great lump that dominates the surrounding towns of Bolton and Horwich. Rich in history, evidence of occupation from at least the Bronze Age has been found on its slopes. Always vitally important to the locals, its Mass Trespass predates that on Kinder Scout by a generation. In the late 20th century it not only provides the off-road rider with a magnificent bridleway around its western aspect, but also some fine lanes. It also plays host to fell runners (the Belmont Winter Hill race is run in May), rock-climbers, walkers, horse riders and flyers of elegant, slope-soaring model gliders!

Although there is quite a bit of roadwork, the track around the Pike is not to be missed, and if time is short a quick return to the Blue Lagoon via the Black Dog has much to recommend it! A steady, all-weather route, with level riding off-road – but beware the A675 and A666 if busy.

Route Description

a) – b)

Turn left out of the car park, which commands a magnificent view back towards the village of Belmont, and continue across to the northern flanks of Winter Hill. Steeply uphill, now with the Winter Hill mast to the left, past the sign 'Borough of Chorley', and straight on for 100 metres to the obvious

Belmont (Rivington Pike)

track on the left – just before the road begins its descent. Clearly signed 'concessionary bridleway', it leads across the western flank of Winter Hill. A roughly paved, broad track shortly leads to a wide gate, with a bridleway gate (typically a metre wide with a board at its foot) beside. The accompanying sign proclaims, 'For use by walkers, horses and pedal cyclists.' A truly magnificent track with a firm, stony surface, following the contours around the hill. Only one short muddy patch, this is mountain biking par-excellence! Soon the obvious track presents views west over the train of Rivington reservoirs, and then suddenly, as we round a curve, the unmistakable Pigeon Tower is revealed. Straight on and through a gate near the tower, alongside the rhododendron bushes, on a broad track. Turn left through the gate, heading for the obvious, squat tower of Rivington Pike, following the bridleway signpost. The obvious track zigzags up the hill (ignoring the steps directly to the summit), and leads pleasantly, but not without some effort, around the back of the tower, spiralling to the top of the Pike.

b) – c)

Either descend from the tower by following the rather steep track south to meet the continuation of the previous bridleway, or (preferably) retrace the last 100 metres of ascent and pick up the lower track from there. This leads to a gate with a bridleway sign. Turn left, on to the continuation of the lower track from the Pigeon Tower. Continue straight on, gently down the superb bridleway, past Pike Cottage – 'Grandma Holding's Tea Rooms' – surely an ideal spot to stop if possible. The track becomes metalled, and we shortly meet the Barrow Bridge route where it arrives from the tough little climb from Horwich. As Route 1, we continue for half a mile, then turn left into Matchmoor Lane and along the exposed moorland road to the T-junction. Turn left along the twisty, undulating road until Colliers Row Farm is reached. Here we depart from Route 1 by a left turn into the bridleway, which is well signed immediately after the cottage. The metalled track rises steadily on and past the next farm in 200 metres. Hidden away on the right is the magnificent Brownstones crag – a well-loved bouldering venue. We soon arrive at a T-junction of tracks and turn right – shortly leading to the road, where we turn right. An easy downhill ride leads to Scout Road, at the crossroads. Before leaving Coal Pit Road, however, it would be churlish not to make the 200-metre detour, by a left turn out of the bridleway, to see the fine stone placed 100 years after Britain's first mass-trespass. Back at the crossroads, we turn left and continue along Scout Road as it swings down past Wilton Quarries (another set of well-known crags), to finally reach the Bolton to Blackburn A675 (care!) at a T-junction.

c) – d)

Turn right, heading downhill in the direction of Bolton. Continue pleasantly down (provided it's not too busy) for half a mile, past the Wilton Arms. Soon after, Horrocks Fold is seen on the right and houses begin to displace fields. Turn left down Templecombe Drive. The housing estate has, lamentably, paid little heed to preserving the bridleway, so we follow the line with some difficulty. Continue straight on, down and around the sweeping curves of Templecombe Close, with a TR at the second Midford Drive, (as it forms a loop). Straight on after 100 metres leads along an unmarked path, just before Midford bends right, and near Masbury Close. Continuing straight on past the bollards shortly leads into Springfield Road, where 'No Parking Here' and 'Private Road' signs abound. In 200 metres we pass the car park and back entrance to the Cheetam Arms, then reach the main road at a T-junction. Here we make an acute left turn (care), immediately passing the pub's front entrance.

d) – a)

Continue along the A666 in the direction of Dunscar, as the Darwin Road feeds in from the right. Ignoring signs to 'The Last Drop Village', continue straight on and up the steady rise past the Mason's Arms, through Dunscar. Straight on to Edgerton, past the post office and The Globe, until a happy escape can be made by a left turn, just before the chapel, down Longworth Road.

After the long grind on the A666 this lane provides a welcome contrast, and with some relief we are out to West Pennine Moors country again. Win-

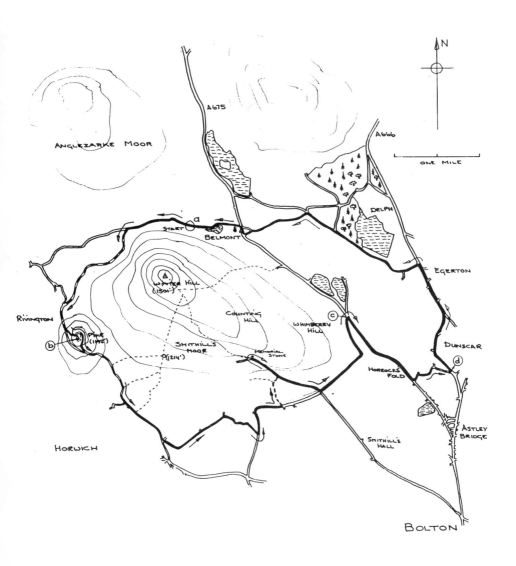

Route 3: Belmont

ter Hill again comes into sight on the left as we continue past Delph Sailing Club on the right. As we progress along this lane the great brooding mass of Winter Hill becomes more evident, now revealing its proliferation of relay masts. The elegant spire of Belmont church can now be discerned, and the strong aroma of the coniferous plantation precedes the junction with the traditional (sadly, now uncommon) cast iron signpost indicating – left to Belmont, Preston 14½, and Bolton back 4½. Turn left then down the steep hill, heading for the bleach works in the dip. Straight on, and exit Edgerton Road where it meets the A675. Turn right in the direction of Blackburn, and in 100 metres we are back in Belmont, with the Black Dog on the corner where we turn left – another good place for refreshments! We follow the sign 'Rivington 3¼, Chorley 7½', up Church Street.

On the corner opposite the Black Dog is a stone trough commemorating Queen Victoria's Diamond Jubilee, 1897. I wonder if she would have been amused by this route – surely possible on a pre-1897 'safety'! Finally, a last great effort up the steep hill past the church and beyond the village, soon returns us to the starting point at the Blue Lagoon car park.

Summary

a) – b)

TL out of car park
SO, steeply uphill
TL into BW (SP)
SO around Winter Hill to Pigeon Tower
TL thro' gate, SP BW (to Rivington Pike)
Follow track to tower

b) – c)

Reverse last part & TR on to main track
SO to gate & T-jn with previous BW
TL, on BW
SO, past Pike Cottage to rd
SO for 1ml
TL into Matchmoor Rd
SO to T-jn
TL, SO to Colliers Row Fm
TL immediately after fm, along BW to BW T-jn
TR & along to T-jn with Coal Pit Rd
TR (for Mass Trespass stone, TL)

c) – d)

TL at Xrds, along Scout Rd
SO to T-jn
TR & along A675
SO, past Wilton Arms, for ½ml
TL into Templecoombe Dr
TR at 2nd Midford Dr
SO along path, past bollards
SO along Spring field Rd

d) – a)

TL & along A666, past Cheetam Arms
SO to Dunscar
SO to Edgerton, past The Globe
TL along Longworth Rd
SO past Delph Sailing Club
TL at SP Belmont, Preston 14½
TR & along A675 for 100m to Belmont
TL along Church Rd, at SP 'Rivington 3¼'
SO past Black Dog & church, steeply uphill
TL into car park.

Route 4 – Ramsbottom

Distance: 15 miles
Off-road: 54%
Height Gain: 1250ft
Time: 2½ – 3½ hours
Start/Finish: Holcombe Moor car park, Holcombe Rd, Ramsbottom (B6214). GR 781 163
Maps: OS Landranger 109, Explorer 19
Rating: *
Grading: Difficult (-)
Gradient: B

'To be able really to see, it is not enough to open the eyes, one must first open one's heart.'
Gaston Rebuffat, Alpiniste, c.1970

Route Summary

This route provides a great deal of interesting riding, although it should not be underrated for rather tricky route finding, or overall height gain. The gradient only failed to achieve 'A' status because this was mostly confined to the roads – nevertheless, good exercise! The bridleways are surprisingly fine, especially considering that they are never far from the town, but some sections (see text) could be prone to being muddy in wet conditions and so the route is best suited to decent weather. It is hard to imagine a better time than a clear summer's evening – but it can be a fine line between enjoying a glorious sunset and getting lost in the dark, especially with the A56 to negotiate!

Route Description

a) – b)

The car park, sited below the Peel Tower, makes a brilliant starting point and fine views across the deep valley presage many more to come, provided the weather is favourable. Turn right out of the car park and along Holcombe Road, gaining a little more height until the road levels out and reaches the outlying gritstone houses of the hillside village of Holcombe – a little gem! Past the Old Post Office, we make an acute left turn immediately before the Shoulder of Mutton. Ignoring the cobbled bridleway going straight on, we follow the narrow lane past Heather Cottage and Smithy Cottage, rising a little – it is tarmac here. Continue straight on, past the Manor House, following the bridleway sign (assuming it points in the right

Bridleway, Holcombe

direction, which it didn't on my journey!). The route is obvious, however, running delightfully down the cobbled lane (thanks to large, not too hard, tyres!), past picturesque cottages and expansive views to the left of our starting point and across the hills to the Central Pennines – we will soon be sampling their delights! Over some small steps and straight on over the lane crossing at Darulaem, following bridleway signs. This fabulous cobbled lane steepens significantly before it finally emerges at the busy junction where the back road from Bolton approaches Ramsbottom.

b) – c)

We make our way across the busy road and turn right to the traffic lights, where we turn left and left again after only 10 metres, heading down Pott Green Lane, thankfully leaving the traffic behind. Gently downhill along the little lane and past the bollards that prevent motors from using this as a through road, to reach Summerseat Lane, running through the housing estate. Continuing pleasantly down, we eventually arrive at a mini-roundabout where we turn left and follow the sweep of the road, taking the second right turn along Railway Street, with signs to Summerseat Garden Centre. Alongside the canal, the road leads to a left turn and a railway bridge, under which we pass. Now we start in earnest the climb up Rowlands Road, past Summmerseat Primary School and Rowlands Methodist church, until the easing of the gradient where we ignore the road off to the right. Instead, we continue straight on, past the 'No Through Road' sign. This leads straight on into a narrow track with a semi-metalled surface – part broken tarmac, part cobbles – dry for me but it could hold puddles if wet. Always an obvious track, it is surprisingly varied as we pass fields and a farm, then back to a row of houses as we suddenly emerge at the busy A56, north of Bury, at the sign 'Public By-Way' and 'Rowlands Road'.

c) – d)

Turn right (with care) and go gently downhill along the A56, through some pleasant, leafy suburbia despite the busy road. At the New Inn (on the right), turn left into Palatine Drive and go through a quiet estate. Taking the second left turn, we go along Lancaster Drive to the T-junction (only a few metres), then turn right and in 50 metres turn left into Mill Road. We keep on the track that runs immediately to the right of the mill, by the iron railings, to the stone wall. Go up past a few houses on a semi-metalled track to reach a junction of tracks. Ignoring the bridleway that runs left, we turn right and then go straight on past Walmsley Conservative Club and down the enclosed, unsurfaced track (ignoring the road that leads right and into the estate).

At the bottom of the track we reach the metalled lane, with 'Redfern Birchell' on the left, opposite a lane on the right. Immediately after the building, a footpath to the left is followed. Note! Obviously we cannot ride this path, but the 200 metre-push up the tarmac-and-cobbles provides a welcome chance to enjoy the improving vista as we leave suburbia for the countryside once more. For anyone intent on riding throughout, a small detour is shown on the map and summary, as only in a special case should a footpath be followed, and certainly never ridden upon. Up the steady climb, with a left turn immediately before the farm into an (unmarked) bridleway. Continue along the fine, unsurfaced track, some 2 metres wide and running between hedges, as it suddenly carries us safely over the M66. There's always something satisfying about travelling with such freedom over such great roads, with all their restrictions – on speed, direction and movement. On the other side we cross another golf course – I wonder if anyone's ever tried to play across them? The track twists and turns through the golf course, now on a sandy surface, but it finally becomes metalled as it reaches Birchenbower Farm, decoratively adorned with scrap cars. Proceed to Sillinghurst Farm and a T-junction. Turn right, heading east for 100 metres, and then take a sharp left turn up the small lane, heading for open country.

d) – e)

As I gazed back west towards Holcombe, a hot-air balloon drifted effortlessly up the valley and a trio of runners puffed past – what one sees is a function of how one travels!

Up to the junction with the signs from Birtle, ahead to Dingstone and a 'No through road' to the right. Take the acute right turn, running between drystone walls to the farm. Straight on through the metal gate marked 'No motorbikes – horses keep to the bridleway.' The track narrows between the walls, and the gritstone boulders make for interesting riding and pushing. A fine situation, but well-used by horse riders, to whom we must be sure to give way. A flagstone section indicates its likely origins as a packhorse trail – always delectable going! Straight on, uphill and through a gate. The track hugs the hillside as it runs through the heather to reach the tall, white mast at the high point. Continue straight on over the tops and then down the fine track, over the erosion-control plinths at intervals. Continue straight on at the metalled lane (ignoring the bridleway on the right), past the cottages and hotel as the descent steepens. Turn left at Birtle Green Farm and continue easily along the semi-metalled track, keeping left at the fork. The descent leads to woods and a prominent 'No Entry' sign at the cottages at the bottom. Turn right and steeply down the tiny track (could be a little muddy) to the steam crossing at the footbridge. Now, going right at the bottom of the valley, we climb, steeply at first, up the bank on a fine track which could also be tricky if wet. Go up through woodland, following alongside a stream to a stone slab and bear left. This is just about rideable all the way. Across the open field, following the thin track to the wooden gate. Still devoid of signs, we continue straight on, now between hedges, then delightfully downhill to the road, emerging at the first bridleway sign for some time.

e) – f)

Arriving at the apex of the bend, we turn left and begin some roadwork that provides a not unpleasant contrast to the rigours of off-road route-finding. Climb past Leeches Farm and Copped Hill Farm with a fair effort, to reach high ground and a nice run down to the reservoir, where I had the great good fortune to arrive at a glorious sunset, with the Peel Tower silhouetted on the horizon – memorable! At the end of Ashworth Road we turn left at the T-junction, and head west along Edenfield Road, with true Pennine moorland all around. Owd Betts (pub) looks good for rest, otherwise continue, past the 'Lancashire' sign and up another rise. Turn left into the bridleway (signposted), and go along a track shared with Rossendale School. The tarmac track ceases as we continue straight on, where the school road turns right. The excellent, if rather stony, track leads to a cobbled lane and semi-metalled track that continues downhill past the farm. It's cobbled again as we reach Twine Valley Farm and a T-junction – a great run!

f) – a)

Turn left and uphill for 100 metres to suddenly meet the T-junction at the busy A56. Turn left along the main road, with occasional glimpses of the Peel Tower through gaps between the houses on the right. Go straight on past The Packhorse (this is now Whalley Road) and then turn right into Peel Brow, signposted 'Ramsbottom'. Then it's neatly back over the M66 and straight on downhill to the bottom in Ramsbottom, following the sign 'East Lancs Railway' (must try the steam train some day!). Go past the Good Samaritan, Railway Hotel and over the canal bridge and through the heart of Ramsbottom, bedecked with hanging baskets of flowers when I passed. Continue straight on, across Bolton Street, along Market Place and in the direction of the cycleway sign.

Now begins the sting-in -the-tail pull uphill, quite stiffly past the Rose and Crown (tempting!) as the road swings left, easing the gradient. Up again, now as Tanner Street, to gain the top of the rise. Instead of continuing straight on along the level, we turn right, going brutally uphill again, as evidenced by the 25% gradient sign. This proved a rise too steep for my weary legs so I pushed the last bit, past the magnificently sited church set behind the high, stone wall. Shortly we reach the Shoulder of Mutton and recognise the lane opposite as the one up which we began this outing. Turn left at the pub, continuing straight on past the bridleway in 20 metres. It's now mercifully flat, followed by a welcome downhill glide for half a mile, back to the car park – a cracking little route and no soft touch!

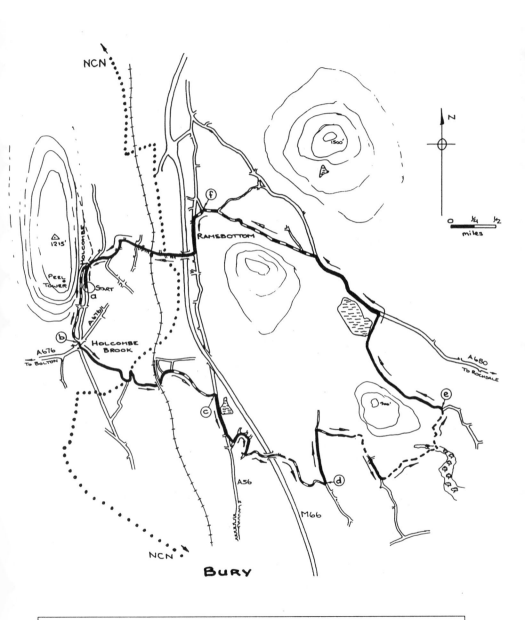

Route 4: Ramsbottom

Summary

a) – b)
TR out of car park, towards Holcombe
TL immed. before Shoulder of Mutton – (acute L, ignoring BW, SO)
SO past Heather Cottage & then Manor House
SO over lane crossing (SP, BW)

b) – c)
TR at main rd, to traffic lights; TL at lights
TL after 10 metres into Pott Green Lane, SO thro' estate
TL at mini-roundabout; 2nd TR along Railway St.; TL & under railway bridge
SO, steeply uphill (Rowlands Rd)
SO into BW (SP 'No Thro' Rd'); SO past fm, under pylons, to A56

c) – d)
TR along A56; TL opposite New Inn into Palatine Rd
2nd TL into Lancaster Dr.; TR (after a few metres)
TL (after 50m) into Mill Rd; TR (ignoring BW SP L)
SO past Walmsley Cons. Club
TL immed past Redfern Birchell, at bottom of hill – N.B. footpath – must not ride!
TL into BW track immed before fm
SO, over M66; SO, to Sillinghurst Fm

d) – e)
TR; TL (after 100m)
TR (acute) at jn (SP – 'Birtle', 'Dingstone', 'No Thro' Rd')
SO past fm (along BW); SO, uphill & past white mast; SO down lane
TL at Birtle Green Fm; keep L at fork, SO to end main track, to 'No Entry' sign
TR into narrow path (BW) thro' woods – steeply down
SO, over small bridge across stream
SO along indistinct BW – steeply up; TL at rd (apex of bend)

e) – f)
SO past Leeches Fm, uphill!
SO past Resr. (Ashworth Rd)
TL at T-jn, along Edenfield Rd
SO past Owd Betts; TL into BW (SP 'Rossendale School')
SO along BW to T-jn. (Twine Valley Fm.)

f) – a)
TL & in 100m TL & along A56
SO, past Pack Horse
TR (SP 'Ramsbottom'), along Peel Brow
SO, over M66
SO, downhill, over level crossing
SO past Railway Hotel
SO along Market Place
SO, uphill, Tanner St.
TR, past '25%' gradient SP, past Holcombe Church
TL at Shoulder of Mutton
SO, flat (!), then downhill to car park; TL into car park.

The Central Pennines

This area epitomises, for me, Lancashire and its by-ways. Rugged, no nonsense, dark-weathered gritstone; black, peaty-soft moorland; and towns clustering in the valley bottoms – leaving lonely footpaths and bridleways to feel their tenuous way up and over the moors, linking town to town, Red to White Rose.

The geographical distinctions are largely of my own making, for strictly the West Pennine Moors extend east into this section, and the Central Pennines continue, of course, into West and North Yorkshire. These are routes that have a Central Pennine 'feel' to them. All around are close links between the hand (mostly Victorian) of man and nature. Hollingworth Lake, developed as a fashionable 19th-century holiday centre, was pivotal in transport evolution. This region around Littleborough was important as a trans-Pennine route to the industrial West Riding, being in the vanguard of developments in canals (hence the lake), railways, and finally motorways, with the M62 flying 140ft above the valley floor at Rakewood Viaduct, (under which we pass on Route 6!).

Preceding all these were the ancient packhorse trails and turnpike roads. 'Perhaps the most remarkable surviving Roman road in England,' was how the doyen of landscape archaeologists, W.G. Hoskins, described the dramatic descent from the 'Aggin Stone' on Blackstone Edge, towards Littleborough. The ancient track, packhorse trail, turnpike road and modern A58 all find different routes over the summit of an edge described by Daniel Defoe in the 18th century as, 'the English Andes'. Now it's even traversed by the Pennine Way. On a fine day we can enjoy these routes from Hollingworth Lake without qualms – Defoe unwisely chose a snowstorm and contemporary transport for his epic journey!

The sprawling conurbations of Rochdale, Burnley and Blackburn were formed in the heat of the Industrial Revolution, in the same manner as Bolton and Bury, of the previous section. But growth was largely confined to the valleys as the mills were first sited by the rivers. Initially powered by waterwheel, when the steam age arrived these sites were often found to be convenient for the local coal measures. This left the surrounding moors intact, rising steeply from the valleys, and the hillside hamlets of the handloom weavers were mostly left in a state of arrested development.

From Rochdale there is continuous ribbon development northwards up the valley to Whitworth. But here we can suddenly escape to the moors, up the ancient packhorse trail right over Rooley Moor, and down to the Rossendale Valley on the far side. Similarly, from Burnley we travel east, steeply up to the 1000ft contour, to find a scattering of villages that have a shape recognisable from their medieval origins. Worsthorne is a good example, placed just too far from Burnley to get dragged wholesale into the Industrial Revolution, and now featuring may a des. res. for city commuters. Its fine bridleway runs due east over the high moors to Yorkshire, where we can follow for fun a route that was created by hard necessity – although I suspect that it wasn't necessarily all work and no play for the young bloods, even in those days! The ride starts from a convenient car park and picnic site at nearby Hurstwood, a delightful hamlet that retains several venerable stone cottages – reputedly including the home of the Elizabethan poet, Edmund Spenser, author of *The Faerie Queene*.

South of Burnley, the moors and valleys are followed on a variety of bridleways, finishing on Cribden Hill. Although the going is at times tough, it is never unreasonable; and alone on a bike one feels not so far removed from travellers of long ago – until the dubious 'luxury' of an escape back on the A56!

Wycoller is a hamlet that has undergone a remarkable revival. As a born-again 18th-century community, its once neglected fabric now provides sought-after homes; the 'Aisled Barn', an excellent visitor centre; and a cottage café which is a welcome halt. Even the several remarkable bridges spanning its beck have been recovered, after they were swept away in the flash floods that can hit an isolated hamlet within the shadow of the 1700ft Boulsworth Hill. Notably, the thousand-year-old Clam Bridge, one of the oldest in England, has been restored. An isolated community, it supported 350 souls in the boom-time of hand loom weaving, but when the factory system burst the bubble, the residents drifted off to Nelson and Colne, until by 1950 only a single inhabitant remained. Fortunately, local action led to the Council designating the whole area as a country park, and literally saving it from ruin, apart from the hall, of course. Ruined Wycoller Hall was well known by the Brontës and its surroundings undoubtedly figured in their novels – the walk from Haworth being well within their capabilities. We meet the Brontës and their biographer, Elizabeth Gaskell, again in the Lune Valley and Silverdale.

Wycoller's myths are particularly colourful, like the naming of 'Huntsman's Leap', the distinctive gritstone promontory near the Haworth Road. An indicted criminal was reputed to have wagered his liberty against an attempt to leap the gaping chasm on this high outcrop. He succeeded by jumping on his horse, but couldn't stop so they plunged down the hillside to their doom. Tales of ghosts and ill-starred squires surround Wycoller Hall, all described in the visitor centre. History, especially on a quiet winter's day, is not just seen, but felt at Wycoller!

Route 5 – Whitworth

Distance: 12 miles
Off-road: 50%
Time: 2 – 3 hours
Height Gain: 900ft
Start/Finish: North West WaterSki Centre, Whitworth, Rochdale. GR 882 187
Maps: OS Landranger 109, Explorer 19
Rating: *
Grading: Moderate
Gradient: B

'I cannot begin to quantify the inspiration I have had from tramping these miles of open Pennine paths enjoyed since I was young.'
Mike Harding, in his role as President, South Pennines Packhorse Trails Trust.

Route Summary

A good route, possibly typical of the Southern Pennines, with its linear towns in the valley, now rather busy with traffic, and its hamlets encroaching on the moor. Here weavers' cottages can still be recognised by their long line of upstairs windows (often partly infilled). Despite the slightly scrappy initial track, the bridleway improves with height, as it traverses the isolated Rooley Moor. Rideable in most conditions, it can provide superb views, especially on the descent (which requires care) to the Rossendale Valley.

It fails to get more 'stars' because of the need to return by these roads – but with sensible timing this should present no great problem – normal precautions appropriate. Overall – well worth doing for the glorious bridleway – but beware the road!

Route Description

a) – b)

The NW WaterSki car park provides a fine vantage point, looking down over Whitworth. Behind is the reservoir, surrounded by the moors. Exiting from the car park, turn right and go down the hill (up which we will have come earlier), past the Cock and Magpie and then turn right along Cowm Park Way South. This road runs pleasantly along the flat, parallel to the busy main road through Whitworth, past playing fields and a mill, to a junction. Turn right on to The Crescent and go over a small bridge. Go past the mill, Hallfold United Reformed Church and the school as the road gains

Whitworth (Rooley Moor)

height. At the T-junction, turn left along Wallbank Drive. The road continues to gain height in a series of inclines until it runs through the housing estate. Continue straight on to a dirt track (adjacent to number 128), to open
ground, then in 20 metres bear left at the fork, going downhill around the 'S'
bends and the disused building. Some rubbish has been left around here,
but the track is followed as it climbs between stone walls, up a rough track
with the remains of a cobbled surface. Whilst this is locally used by all and
sundry and is waste ground, the initial 200 metres of the track from the road
is not shown as an official Right of Way on the map, so a short and convenient push is a necessary precaution. Go up the paved track and turn right at
the fork where a small hamlet stands. Continue past the attractive cottages
with their cobbled yards and on to a tarmac lane that leads down past the
delightful Waste Cottage, on the apex of the bend. The narrow, high-
banked lane climbs uphill and over a cattle grid to fork right and go past the
row of hill cottages. The unsurfaced track now provides fine views south
over Rochdale and the Pennines. There are numerous grassy mounds, indicative of old mineral workings, a sight often to be seen in the South Pennines. These are often high on the moors, contrasting with the major
housing growth which was concentrated in the valleys as the Industrial
Revolution drew in large numbers of workers to the region.

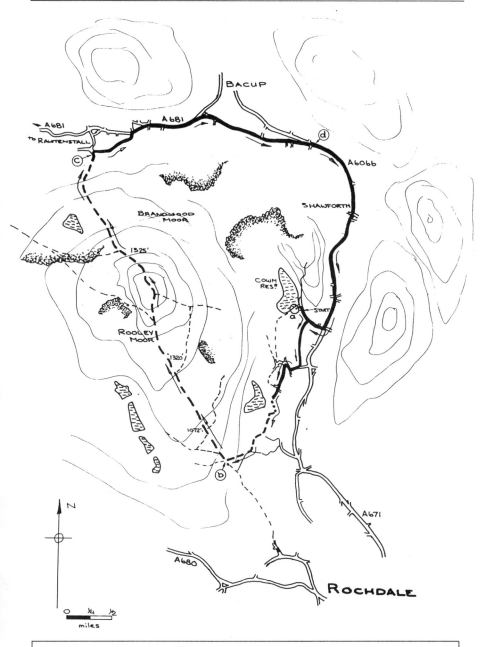

Route 5: Whitworth

b) – c)

The track ends at a T-junction – the way ahead barred by a gate. Turn right here, on the track that has come from the valley, following the magnificent bridleway that will take us right over Rooley Moor and down to the Rossendale Valley, along the Rossendale Way. This is a fine example of an old packhorse trail, one of the best in the area. When I travelled over it the weather was threatening to break and I was prepared for a storm, but instead was rewarded by dramatic skies, with brief bursts of evening sunshine and then a rainbow right at the high plateau – the atmosphere was impressive, yet not intimidating. Our fickle weather does mean that no two trips ever provide quite the same sensation.

From the start the track has a good, stony surface, and is rideable as the gradient is steady, if energetic! In 200 metres we pass under the pylons and the sign 'Rooley Moor – no motor-cycles or motors'. Go straight on past a number of track crossings, a broad track hereabouts. Beyond the section with a loose stone surface, we come to a cobbled section – which is something of a surprise in such an apparently remote place – until we see on 18th-century maps its importance as a trade route, pre-dating the later routes along the valley. There are tremendous views as the track alternates from paved to stony, but still rideable for the energetic. Go over the first top and along some fine paving. Several more tops are breasted , keeping straight on along the main track, before we finally begin the rapid descent to the Rossendale Valley, having experienced a wide variety of paving. There are even some double-row flagstones for a stretch, demonstrating the past traffic which this once saw – how fortunate we are to inherit this solely for leisure use!

As the way down steepens, the track swings off to the left, but we continue straight on down the increasingly stony and rough track. Superb views north up the valleys! On the edge of prudent riding, I found it judicious to dismount for a short section but then it is pure delight – we shortly reach the end of the moor at a gateway which leads straight on over a stream and past a farm. Now the semi-metalled lane leads very steeply down to Rakehead Lane.

c) – d)

Continue past the Alf Kyme factory and turn right at the terraced cottages, going past Lancashire Waste Services and just above the floor of the valley. Blackwood Road finally runs downhill and over the river to meet the main Bacup road at a T-junction opposite the church. Turn right past Gibbs Mew (pub), and along New Church Road. Straight on at the mini-roundabout and past the adjacent eating houses – traditional English café, Chinese chip shop and a Tandoori – a bit of a culture shock after the moors! Continue past the Fairholme Tavern and finally turn right, following the sign 'Rochdale, A6066'.

At the Royal Oak the road begins to rise a little and we fork right, past Bacup Corporation Park and the striking church of St Saviour. The rise continues along New Line and then Park Crescent. Past the New Line Industrial Estate, a fishing pond and the Lancashire Sock Manufacturing Company, an evident survivor of a once-prolific industry. Go straight on as a major road joins from the left. Turn right after the petrol station on Rochdale Road, and past the Travellers' Rest.

d) – a)

In 50 metres, past the sign 'Whitworth – twinned with Kandle', we begin a long, gentle downhill to the town centre. When I passed through, the flower pots were blooming on the wide grass verge beside the road and the air filled more with the strong aroma of cut grass than diesel – visitors from Kandle would have received a good impression that evening. I was probably fortunate, at a quiet time on the roads, but under such conditions the route is not unpleasant, although it looks rather fearsome on the map. Moral: avoid the rush hour and freight!

On a road now surprisingly well named as Moorland View, we continue past the Red Lion on a cycle lane. Go past the post office, and we have possibilities for contriving a parallel route along the back lanes – although it seemed unnecessary on my trip. A linear town, Whitworth stretches like a ribbon alongside the stream along the valley towards a distant Rochdale. The road changes from Millgate Terrace to Market Street, then past the Half Way House to Parker Square.

We finally turn right into Tong Lane, following the sign 'BDWSA, Whitworth Water Ski Centre'. The turning is easily missed, evident if the Rawstron Arms is reached 100 metres further on. Go straight on down the road and shortly back to the Cock and Magpie, where we bear right and uphill to return to the centre.

Summary

a) – b)

TR out of Water Ski car park & downhill
SO, past Cock & Magpie
TR at Cowm Park Way South
TR at T-jn
SO along The Crescent, past Hallfield Church
TL at T-jn, along Wellbank Dr
SO thro' housing est.

b) – c)

SO, alongside no.128, into track
SO, thro' waste ground (dismount along track)
bear L at fork after 20m
SO downhill, then uphill over cobbles
TR at fork (hamlet)
SO, some tarmac, small lane, past Waste Cottage
SO up track, past grassy mounds
TR at T-jn with cobbled BW
SO along the long BW, over Rooley Moor to Rossendale Valley
SO, down tricky descent

c) – d)

TR after Alf Kyme factory
SO past Lancs. Waste Services, over bridge to T-jn
TR opp. church & Gibbs Mew, & along Newchurch Rd
SO at mini-roundabout
TR, following SP 'Rochdale A6066'
fork R after Royal Oak
SO past Bacup Park & St.Saviour's Church
SO, along New Line & Park Cres.
TR at main Rochdale Rd

d) – a)

SO, past Travellers Rest & into Whitworth
SO, along Moorland View, Market St, & past Red Lion & Halfway House
TR at SP 'BDWSA – Whitworth Water Ski Centre' into Tong Lane
SO, over Cowm Park Way South
bear R at Cock & Magpie & cont. uphill
TL into start.

Route 6 – Hollingworth Lake

Distance: 8 miles
Off-road: 75%
Height Gain: 850ft
Time: 1 – 2 hours
Start/Finish: Hollingworth Lake, marine centre car park, or Visitors Centre. GR 933 150
Maps: OS Landranger 109, Outdoor Leisure 21
Rating: *
Grading: Moderate (-)
Gradient: B

'I must now turn the course of my journey another way, unto the rest of the Brigantes ... and first into Lancashire which I go unto (God speed me well) after a sort somewhat against my will.'
William Camden, 17th-century chronicler (travelling across the Pennines from Yorkshire)

Route Summary

A fine route in a fascinating area that provides a remarkable array of transport history 'on the ground' (and water!). Well worth further visits to explore the excellent walks and sights, although it is perhaps at its best at off-peak times. A short route, ideal for a late start on a fine evening, it could also be suitable for a first off-road outing where something a little more challenging than flat cycleways is sought, dismounting on steep descents. The surfaces are generally excellent, but winter conditions could make Clegg Moor unsuitable for an easy ride.

Route Description

a) – b)

From the marine centre car park, turn right and pass the various eating establishments as we head towards the impressive viaduct, a mile distant, that carries the M62 over the Pennines and into Yorkshire. Keeping right, we trace the edge of the lake, going past the Fisherman's Inn (est.1800), following the sign 'Rakewood ¾'. Off to the left is the alternative start of the Visitors Centre – ideally placed to start a variety of delightful walks and rides that this attractive area has to offer. The area is truly rich in local history and offers a microcosm of British transport which is second to none.

As the road swings right, towards the lake, we continue straight on and up the track, following the bridleway signpost. Initially paved, the good track leads past the Warden's Cottage and into a semi-metalled lane that finally reaches the imposing Sykes House, at the beginning of the moor. Go straight on along the good track, over the cattle grid and up the hill as it gradually reduces to a single, stony track. It swings right to meet the dry-stone wall, then we turn left (following the markers) and make a rising traverse of the hillside, following a narrow path. It finally emerges on the broad track that runs around the hill, parallel to the pylons – rather spoiling the otherwise grand vista. Turn left along the main track.

b) – c)

For reference, we actually join the main track at the third pylon from the M62 (which lies hidden in a cutting a few hundred metres to the right). This is Clegg Moor, which we now skirt around, and the route is well marked. Continue pleasantly down the gentle slope – a favourite for horse riders – and straight on to meet the metalled lane, following the yellow marker. This leads over the cattle grid and easily to Lydgate. At the junction with signs to Hollingworth, Rakewood and Blackstone Edge, we turn right to follow the latter. After 50 metres, through the de-limit signs to the attractive cottages set high above the stream and road, providing rather spectacularly steep rock gardens! Steeply up and we soon reach the crossing of the A58 Littleborough to Blackstone Edge road that runs across the Pennines into Yorkshire. The Cottage at this crossing displays 'Blackstone Edge Old Road'. We simply cross (with care!) the A58 and follow the bridleway sign directly up the hill, on a good track. Around a curve, a hidden pool is revealed, and then at the top of the hill (not as far as it looks!) The White House is prominent. The views are tremendous as we puff up to a well-earned pause at the vantage point of the pub, which forms our high-point.

c) – d)

A few metres further west is the summit of this road and the northern leg of the Pennine Way. We turn right and head off down the A58, shortly passing the Pennine Way on its route south. It's well worth leaving the bike here for the half-mile trot around the contours towards Blackstone Edge, where the legendary Roman road can still be followed to Lydgate. Further up the hillside is the Aggin Stone, an ancient waymarker on an important way over the Pennines. Seventeenth-century travellers such as the indomitable Celia Fiennes and, later, Daniel Defoe were rather awestruck by the crossing, no doubt encountering bad weather on horseback. Defoe even compared the crossing to that of the Andes! In fine weather this is a wonderful spot.

The ride down the A58 is, despite its main road status, enjoyable. No need to pedal for what seems miles, this is payback time for the previous slog uphill! Turn left at the cottage and back along Blackstone Edge Old Road, still freewheeling. Retracing our outward route, continue straight on up the bridleway across Clegg Moor, ignoring the lane which runs off to the right. Continue along the fine track in the line of the pylons, past our earlier entry point, and to the end of this track at the farm – ahead lies the M62.

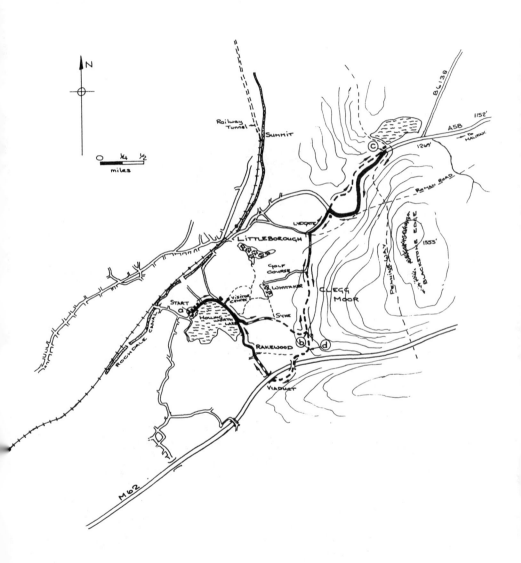

Route 6: Hollingworth Lake

Hollingworth Lake (Clegg Moor)

d) – a)

Go through the gate and the farmyard and we then turn left and over the bridge far above the motorway. Tufn right at the far side and go down the steep, semi-metalled bridleway to the stream at the bottom of a rather delightful, hidden valley – yet so near to the vanished M62! The descent is excellent – but reliable brakes (or an ejector seat) are vital. The track now leads most pleasantly down to swing under the vast span of the M62 Rakewood Viaduct, with great views from its enormous pillars over Hollingworth Lake to the marina.

An easy roll down to the road and through Rakewood leads back past our initial bridleway entry, and we can now bowl along the last half mile around the lake and back to the start, with refreshments galore!

Summary

a) – b)

TR out of marina car park
keep R at SP 'Rakewood ¾', past Fisherman's Inn
SO past Visitors Centre, around lake
TL into BW (SP)
SO, past Warden's Cottage to Sykes House
SO along BW, following SP to main track

b) – c)

TL down main track, around Clegg Moor
SO, down to lane, yellow arrow SP, to Lydgate
TR at jn (SP 'Blackstone Edge')
SO up rd past cottages to A58 (Blackstone Edge Old Rd)
SO over A58 into BW
SO uphill to The White House

c) – d)

TR and down A58
TL at cottage on outward route
SO, return on BW, Clegg Moor
SO to fm, before M62

d) – a)

TR at fm, thro' yard
TL and over M62
TR, steeply down
SO, under Rakewood Viaduct (M62)
SO to lane at Rakewood
SO, around lake to start.

Route 7 – Piethorn Valley

Distance: 15 miles
Off-road: 51%
Height Gain: 1250ft
Time: 2½ – 3½ hours
Start/Finish: Piethorn Valley Reservoir car park, Newhay, GR 953 122.
Alternatively, Newhay Station.(off A640).
Maps: OS Landranger109, Outdoor Leisure 21
Rating: **
Grading: Difficult (-)
Gradient: B

'Wherever you walk on the hills and valleys of the Peak and Pennines – you walk on the bones
of those who have been there before you – from Roman legions to itinerant packmen ... and if
you listen carefully enough you can hear their voices still singing in the wind.'
Mike Harding, Walking the Peak and Pennines, 1992.

Route Summary

This is a tremendous route and well worth two stars! Once again I was fortunate with a glorious Saturday afternoon in high summer. With fine conditions the views are superb, as you gain (and lose!) height rapidly whilst
visiting several reservoirs in the area. It reaches a high point of the Pennines with remarkably little pain, and then crosses the Pennine Way south of
Blackstone Edge, (see previous route).

The scenery, position and quality of bridleways earn this status. Although perhaps a bit stiff for the beginner or supremely unfit, it shouldn't
take long to make the grade to have a bash. It's well worth waiting for decent
weather as the track up Windy Hill could become muddy in places – and it
would be a shame to miss the view – or go astray on the moors!

Route Description

a) – b)

The car park, although ideally situated by the reservoir, and with attached
toilet block, is small and well enclosed by sturdy, stone walls, in keeping
with the area. Alternative parking is possible further up the lane, or even
better, alight from the train at Newhay, a half-mile away. Turn right out of
the car park and go gently downhill past the reservoir and P.W. Greenhalgh's factory, to make an acute right turn, back past the factory on a metalled lane. At the end of the tarmac the continuation around the back of the

Piethorn Valley (heading for Windy Hill)

factory is barred by a gate. We continue straight on, up the super cobbled track, a stiff but rideable rise which winds around and becomes a gravel surface as it passes the white house at the top of the bank. Go straight on and past Higher Rough Bank Farm, soon followed by the converted barn called, remarkably, Higher Rough Bank Barn! Over the rise and the dip takes us straight on and through Rough Farm, ignoring the bridleway off left. Along the obvious track, between drystone walls, and with just an occasional puddle. Ignoring the concrete track to the left, our route runs delightfully down a narrow, drystone-walled track, which soon becomes paved with cobbles. In 50 metres it reaches a junction of tracks. Ahead, barely half a mile away is the M62, although it is surprisingly unobtrusive.

Turn right and up the fine walled-track heading for the farm further up the hill, now running parallel to the westbound M62. This is absorbing riding. Some light mud may be encountered, but in decent conditions there is never sufficient to prove a problem – any wet patches are easily avoided with a modicum of cunning. Straight on past Carr Farm, where the combination of stony surface and incline encourage a push – and a chance to better appreciate the surroundings. The improving track profile soon permits pedalling as we continue straight on past a track that goes left and under the motorway. In 200 metres go through a good gate, now with grand views over the reservoirs and our starting point. This superb bridleway passes a yellow waymarker arrow on a green background, and a sign for the South Pennine Chain. Continue straight on, climbing steadily, and in 150 metres ride under the pylons. Only a couple of easily avoided muddy patches were met – this is a real connoisseur's ride.

b) – c)

At the junction of tracks we turn left (the right providing an alternative of a shorter, less demanding ride appropriate for poor conditions or off-season). From the distinctive stone gateposts (*sans* gates) the fine, grassy track swings upwards, alongside the drystone wall. We now encounter a deep gully where the overgrown track at the bottom is less than inviting – but fortunately, a thin path can be followed high up the bank, providing an excellent test of one's riding prowess! Eventually we descend as the track becomes more conventional, running alongside the high moorland wall where I found a profusion of butterflies and dragonflies. Reach the end of the wall at a gatepost. Continue straight on along the track through a cleft, with occasional sight of the M62 to the left.

Over the rise, down the slope, around some mud, and begin the last climb towards the mast on the high point of Windy Hill – not difficult to imagine how it got its name. A good proportion of the ground can be covered in the saddle and the surface is often most accommodating as we follow the obvious, albeit unmarked, way to the mast. But poor visibility could make route-finding difficult up here. The views are stunning from this vantage point. Press on, up the final rise, passing to the left of the mast. A broad, sandy track leads along the level and past the small car park to the road in 200 metres. Accompanied by the croaking of grouse, we reach the road and a bridleway sign pointing back to Bleaked Gate.

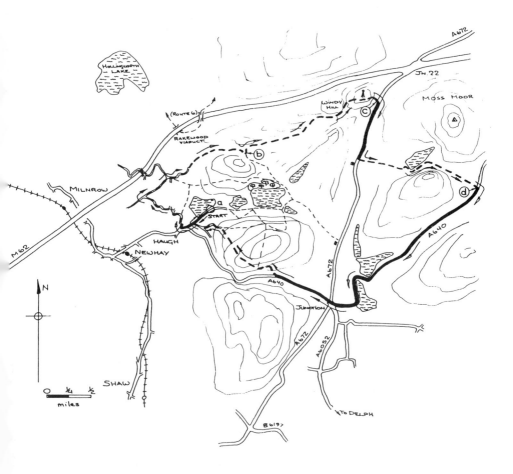

Route 7: Piethorn Valley

c) – d)

Turn right and go along the road, rising a little before descending past the sign 'West Yorkshire', then 'Saddleworth, Oldham'. It's pleasant riding along this open road, with flax on the moor and wide views as we pass the Pennine Way, from Standedge. Down through the 'S' bends, and just before it steepens past the Ram's Head, we turn left. Some 75 metres before the reservoir, the wide gate (next to a narrow one) gives access to the excellent bridleway but, surprisingly, no signpost, apart from 'horses only'. Continue, overlooking the reservoir and the lower one further right, through a gate in 200 metres. Contouring round the hillside on the fine stony/grass track we are confronted with the grass bank of the upper reservoir, previously hidden. Superb riding here. Across the head of the reservoir, we turn left and follow its far side, hard by the stone wall. Along a more stony path beyond the reservoir, over the hill and then a very pleasant ribbon of track as it traces its way down to the road. Here I met an elderly rider of a tourer taking a short cut over the moors instead of the long way around the roads – which somehow seemed to epitomise the freedom of the hills in good conditions.

d) – a)

Exiting from the bridleway at the good gate, we turn right and head off rapidly downhill again – around the sweeping bends, and across the reservoirs. Straight on to the crossroads at the Junction Inn. This is actually called Junction, appropriately, where we cross the A670 Halifax to Oldham road, and head straight on along the A640, Rochdale Road. Leaving Junction we continue along the straight road, past Chapel Cottage Hotel. As we begin a steady climb, a turn right into a bridleway is made. Well-signposted, the track runs alongside the Italian restaurant. After 50 metres the track becomes rather overgrown and suffers a little from the zeal of the adjacent house renovations, but a short push takes us to the farm at the top of the rise. Turn left, around the back of the farm and along a good gravel track. I found some magnificent foxgloves amongst the debris on the way up. We bear right at the fork, ignoring the bridleway that leads left, back to the road. Go straight on and across the moor, heading for the pylons. Over the rise and quite steeply down the well-defined track to reach the metalled lane at the hamlet with 'Shippon 1710' on one of the well-restored cottages grouped around a quadrangle.

We continue steeply down the little lane to pass Lane Bottom Co-op, and the inviting Bull's Head. Turn right 50 metres beyond the pub, and we are back into the lane from Newhay. In 200 metres the car park is reached – a great ride!

Summary

a) – b)

TR out of Resr. car park

TR after P.W. Greenhalgh factory

SO behind factory and up cobbled BW

SO past white house and Higher Rough Bank Fm

SO past Rough Fm

SO to cobbled BW

TR at BW jn

SO past Carr Fm

TR at BW jn

SO along main track, follow yellow signs

b) – c)

TL at BW T-jn

SO, above deep cleft

SO, main track to Windy Hill

TR behind mast, and 200m to rd, past car park

c) – d)

TR along rd

SO over rise and downhill to steep rd before Ram's Head

TL into (unmarked) BW, ('Horses only' sign)

SO to Resr.

TL at far side of Resr.

SO uphill and down to rd – exit BW

d) – a)

TR at rd

SO downhill to Junction

SO along Rochdale Rd (A640), past Junction Inn

SO past Chapel Hotel

TR (BW – SP) by Italian restaurant

SO to fm

TL behind fm

bear R at fork

SO, steeply down

SO to lane, past 'Shippon 1710' cottage

SO down to Bull's Head

TR, retracing route from start, 200m

TL into car park.

Route 8 – Oswaldtwistle Moor

Distance: 10 miles
Off-road: 63%
Height Gain: 650ft
Time: 1½ – 2 hours
Start/Finish: Car park/picnic site on A677, SE of Blackburn (Blackburn – Haslingden road). GR 743 254
Maps: OS Landranger 103, Explorer 19
Rating: *
Grading: Moderate
Gradient: B

> 'Walking has surpassed beer as the shortest cut in our day out of Manchester.'
> *Prof. J.E.M. Joad, 1946*

Route Summary

Surprisingly good value for an unprepossessing route – the bridleways are generally well marked, easy to follow and in a good state of preservation, most encouraging to find in an area that is so closely tied to its industries. The built-up valley is soon quitted and the tracks provide many fine viewing points – although even from the car park it is pretty good!

Neither very strenuous or long, the route makes a good evening outing, and should be fine in most conditions. The roadwork does need a little care as far as route-finding and traffic are concerned, but I found it no problem in the evening, and had time to enjoy a long sunset from the car park whilst trying to identify the hills – like Ingleborough, 32 miles, and Pendle, a mere 11miles – from the plinth.

Route Description

a) – b)

Turn right out of the superbly situated car park, overlooking the towns in the valley and framed by a distant Pendle. Pleasantly along the road, with expansive views right towards Pendle. You reach Ye Olde Brown Cow after about a mile. Turn left immediately before the restaurant, into the good track. Although marked by a prominent wooden signpost, it has no inscription! Going past the house and through a gate, we continue straight on along the semi-metalled track and past the farm in 200 metres. Here, in the evening, I was greeted by the dashing house martins at Meadowside Cottage. Go straight on through a couple of gates at the farm and into the fields.

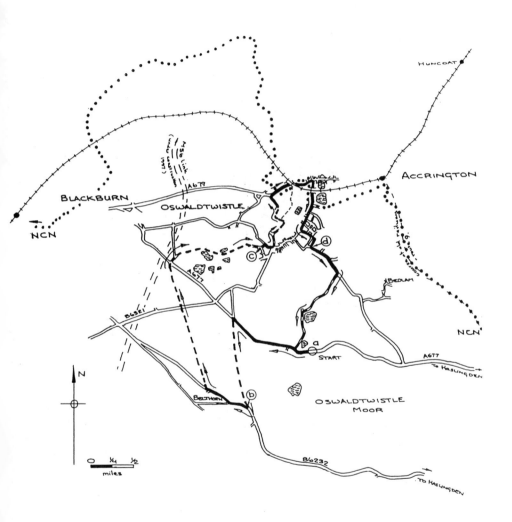

Route 8: Oswaldtwistle

There's another gate after 50 metres, another in a further 50 metres, and yet another, still heading straight up the slope and over the rise. Beyond the farm the way is marked by an overgrown ditch-cum-cleft, so that comparatively easy progress (pushing) is maintained by following alongside the cleft until the rise is breasted and we can drop back into the gully to pass through the gate. This has the characteristics of a 'holloway', an ancient track which makes a deep cleft where the surface has been worn away over the centuries. Along the walled track for 200 metres, riding again, to the farmhouse near the road. The excellent cinder track continues through gates, and in 100 metres reaches the road.

b) – c)

Turn right and along the road, shortly passing under the line of pylons. On the left horizon the Darwin Tower can be seen as we crest a rise and sweep around a bend, and the road descends gently to the Dog Inn. Before reaching the pub, however, we turn right into the clear track on the right, with a green bridleway signpost, although this time its lettering has almost vanished. Heading down the bridleway on a gentle slope, we now have the distant Pendle directly ahead. Straight on through the gate and along the easy track for 50 metres to pass the house and a gate. Continue down the cracking track and past the farm, with the obligatory barking dog – not exactly remarkable as I can't recall a single farmyard without this accoutrement! Straight on down the unmade track, becoming semi-metalled as it finally emerges straight on over a little lane, following the 'bridlepath' signpost. Ride past some cottages and under the pylons along an excellent, semi-metalled path that leads under the motorway (under construction on my visit).

Continue straight on across the lane, only 25 metres from the M65 extension which is due to open late '97. Thankfully the bridleway (not for the first time) has survived the onslaught of the civil engineers. Pleasantly along past a house and spreading chestnut tree, then through a gate by the farm building and out to a small lane. Back on the track it is easily followed around curves as it runs rightwards and under the pylons again. Excellent! The track becomes single line as it follows the stream, then goes along a stony ribbon by the drystone wall. Go straight on through the genuine bridleway gate, gentle inclines and declines make ideal riding. Through another gate – this time constructed from 'inch by eighth' (flat metal strip) which, laid on-edge is not particularly visible, especially in the evening! Finally, we emerge into a back lane to Brookside Industrial Estate, to the strong aroma of TCP! The bridleway sign at our exit points back to Brookside Lane. An unexpectedly pleasant ride.

c) – d)

Go down the lane to the crossing and turn left, and then in 50 metres turn

Oswaldtwistle (first bridleway)

right at the T-junction. Straight on past Elsie's Café to the Black Dog. Continue straight on over the mini-roundabout and along Union Rd. Turn left immediately after the Rose and Crown and along White Ash Lane to its end (¼ml). We continue straight on down the path from the signpost noting 'West End, ½, Harvey St.' Although unsurfaced the way is obvious – between the fences and alongside the housing estate. Keep right at the fork. Left at the next fork, following the fence alongside the allotments, then down a little, over a stream. Through the tunnel and up to 20 metres of tarmac preceding the cobbles. Not unpleasant going - quite a rural atmosphere, although we're in the middle of the town!

Finally, out to the lane and up to Burns Ave. Straight on to the T-junction and turn right along Browning Ave. to another T-junction – turn right again. Exit Thwaites Rd after 50 metres, at the T-junction with the main road. Turn right and head downhill, alongside the canal and under the railway bridge to the middle of Ostwaldtwistle. Turn right along the B6231, following the sign to the town centre and railway station (an opportunity to do the route using only the railway is to be encouraged). Underneath the railway again, straight on past half-a-dozen left turns, The Tavern, Oswaldtwistle Mill and the Foxhill, to turn left along Lord St. (one-way). Continue straight on, now along Sun St., over the crossing and past the church on the right. Turn right at the T-junction and go over the crossing to the T-junction with the main road.

d) – a)

Turn left and immediately begin the long uphill climb – past (?) the Stop and Rest and the end of the park, gaining height steadily. On past The Plough, ignoring the bridleway sign. Go straight on at the mini-roundabout, along Fielding Lane, which then becomes Broadfield Rd and leads past Broadfield School. The hill is unrelenting. Immediately after Greystones House on the right, we turn right down Pothouse Lane, leaving the road still with half a mile to its summit.

The fine, metalled lane leads down and past Oldfield Farm and a sign 'Hoyle Bottom'. Proceed straight on past the houses in the bottom, and up the rise past Cockerly Farm to fine views, left and right. Go straight on over the stream and a reservoir that lies hidden to the left. After the fine stone house, a T-junction of tracks is reached. Turn left and go up the steady slope on a stony surface that proves rideable – the end is not far away! The reservoir is revealed from this position, as the excellent track levels off before reaching the road, also passing another useful parking area. Now metalled, the lane soon arrives at the T-junction with the main road. Turn left and along the A677 for 50 metres, past a sign 'Picnic Site 300yds'. We arrive in more like 150 metres to turn left into the start. Fine – time for another!

Summary

a) – b)

TR out of car park, along A677 for 1ml.

TL into BW, before Ye Olde Brown Cow (SP)

SO up BW, past fm, numerous gates

SO over hill to fm and rd

b) – c)

TR along rd & downhill

TR into BW, before Dog Inn (SP)

SO down gentle slope

SO across lane, under M65, pylons, long BW to town

c) – d)

SO, Brookside Lane

TL, up for 50m

TR & past Black Dog

SO at mini-roundabout (Union Rd)

TL immed. after Rose & Crown (White Ash Lane)

SO to BW SP (Harvey St, West End ½)

SO along BW past estate

R at fork, L at fork, over stream, thro' tunnel

SO & up Burns Ave TR at T-jn

TR at T-jn

TR at T-jn, along main rd, under railway

TR at T-jn (B6231), under railway

SO past several turnings, to Foxhill pub

TL (Lord St)

SO (continues as Sun St), SO at crossing

d) – a)

TL at main rd, long uphill

SO, past Stop & Rest

SO, past mini-roundabout (now Fielding Lane, to Broadfield Rd)

SO, past Broadfield School

TR down BW (Pothouse Lane)

SO past Hoyle Bottom

TL at BW jn, uphill to lane & rd jn

TL along A677, cont. for 150m

TL into start

Route 9 – Huncoat

Distance: 14 miles
Off-road: 36%
Height Gain: 850ft
Time: 2 – 3 hours
Start/Finish: Mill Hill car park, Huncoat, nr. Accrington. GR 786 308
Maps: OS Landranger 103, Explorer 19
Rating: *
Grading: Difficult (-)
Gradient: B

'The valley is gone and the Gods with it ...'
John Ruskin, 19th century, on the coming of the railway to Monsal Dale.

Route Summary

We are now in deep Lancashire. This is true Lancashire Central Pennines, perhaps the next step in a progression, both geographically and in difficulty, to Rawtenstall, the next route. I was pleasantly surprised by the standard of the bridleways. On an unpromising and dull Sunday, I found the pull up to Great Hameldon quite reasonable – a rather scrappy start succeeded by some fine moorland tracks, just sufficiently isolated to be interesting, but without real exposure. The concessionary bridleway from Baxendon to Accrington is most pleasant (one in the eye for Ruskin!).

Overall, it doesn't deserve more stars because of the inevitable roadwork, and I count myself a little fortunate in passing through a quiet Accrington so easily – if without local knowledge, it is best to choose a quiet time through the town. A good choice of route if one has easy access to Accrington. Finally, I found myself feeling rather uninspired by the start – which is entirely unfair to this convenient picnic site – one is hopelessly spoilt by Lancashire's brilliant starting places!

Route Description

a) – b)

Turn left out of the car park and up the steady rise, leading high over the A56(T), up a little further before descending to the T-junction at Huncoat. Exiting Burnley Lane, we turn left into Higher Gate and immediately go past the White Lion, then downhill to the Griffin's Head and the T-junction. Before the coming of the trunk road, the track opposite led directly up to

Great Hameldon (1343ft), but now we need a minor diversion to reach it – Ruskin, I suspect, would not have been amused.

Turn left along Burnley Rd to the first roundabout, going straight on under the A56(T) to the second roundabout, where we take the last exit – the (unmarked) new lane that winds up the hill between the quarry and the trunk road. A small track tunnelling under the A56 looked promising, but has been clearly made out-of-bounds, never mind! The steep, metalled track soon provides good views over the A56 and west. As the quarry is passed the track becomes (surprise!) unsurfaced, but perfectly OK for riding. Bearing left, the track runs up between some rather decrepit drystone walling, under the pylons and past some erratically scattered farm build-

ings on the left. Ignoring the main track which leads left to the farm, we continue straight on, past the boulders, and in 50 metres reach the collapsing gate, complete with barbed-wire. Continue straight on along the stony track and under the telegraph wires to the top of the hill. We follow the track without difficulty in route finding, enjoying some pleasant riding – the track runs alongside a wall and twists in accord with the map. Through another sad gate and a delightful deep cleft making a single line. This was dry on my journey, but hoofprints show its popularity and

Huncoat (bridleway at Accrington)

it could be muddy off-season. Now an enjoyable descent, past the occasional, innocuous patch of mud and through a superb little gorge, still rideable, with water trickling down its rocky bed.

b) – c)

We run out to a parting of the ways where the walls diverge at a triangular patch of rough grass. Take the left fork, then go right at the first opportunity, down a narrow track that deposits one (safely!) on the main track that runs by walls past Higher Hey Farm, over to the right. The A56 can now be seen running parallel on the right, 100 metres away. Enjoy great riding down in the rocky gully, as the track improves to a stony surface and winds down through old workings and past the single, 4ft-high, standing stone. Go up to a metalled lane then straight on to the next tarmac track, where we turn left towards the buildings below the reservoir. Turn right in 50 metres, before reaching them, following the small tarmac lane. The A56 is a half-mile to the right, as we keep right at the junction. Past the farm and the isolated hamlet, then straight on across the larger road to the next hamlet, with a sign 'Sherfin Nook'. Down to the fork, keeping right, as we head down the valley and glimpse the McDonalds at the A56 roundabout, a million miles away. As we continue down, the town of Haslingden can be seen creeping up the far hillside. Eventually a steep descent leads to a junction, Clough End Rd, where we turn right and continue steeply downhill, around a curve. In 50 metres reach the traffic lights at the bottom of the valley.

c) – d)

Straight on at the lights, over the A680 and to a T-junction in 100 metres. Exit Brooke St. by a turn right. Continue straight on, shortly over the A56(T), making a right turn into Rising Bridge Rd. Keeping round to the right at the junction, we now follow Round Hill Lane, going over the bridge and down to the T-junction with the main road. Leaving Worsley St., we turn left along the main road and shortly past the Hollands Pie factory – if the plans of the council come eventually to fruition, it will enable our next bridleway to be extended back to here, a useful prospect! (See Sustrans NCN).

We continue along Manchester Rd, past Baxenden Methodist Church, up the hill and towards the church with the impressive tower in the distance. When I rode here on a Sunday afternoon the road was no problem, but should it be insufferably busy, an escape along the back roads to the right is possible. Just before the church, we pass Baxenden Conservative Club, opposite the Bay Horse.

d) – e)

Turn left here, down Hurstead St., past the school on a semi-metalled lane. Strictly this has footpath status, so a short push is in order, although it is well-used by motors as the only access to the scattering of houses at the bot-

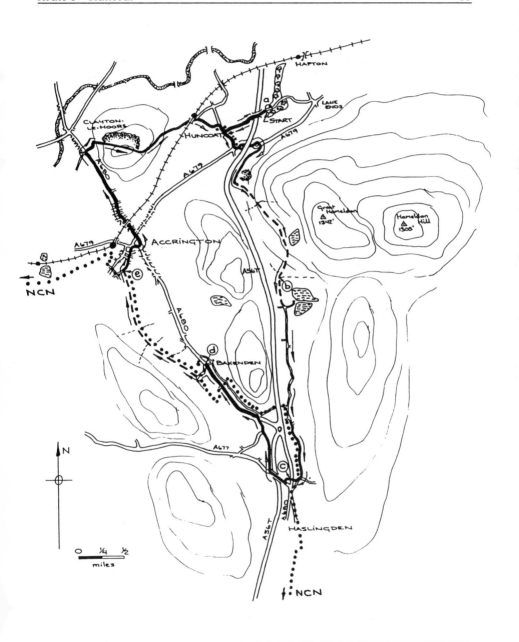

Route 9: Huncoat

tom. Go down to meet the line of the defunct railway, onto which we now turn, (right). Gaining the line, we are afforded a good view through the trees of the church spire in Baxenden, before enjoying the superb track that takes us straight into Accrington. Fine riding - the route is obvious with young silver birches are springing up alongside the line, making it feel quite rural. Near the end are a series of cross-timbers, that are no problem at an appropriate speed. All too soon (for this is the last off- road part), we arrive at the road, suddenly in an urban locale, opposite the Victoria Business Centre. Note that this is a concessionary bridleway, and one should be especially careful, now part of Sustrans National Cycle Network.

e) – a)

Turn right along the road and straight on at the crossing, past the police station and up to the major junction in 100 metres (having come from Spring Gardens and Nuttall St.). Turn left, past Mighty Muldoon's and The Swan, along Abbey St. Continue straight on at the lights, following the sign 'A680'. Continue past The Queens, The Adelphi, and along Eastgate to go straight on through the next lights, signposted 'Huncoat'. At the next lights, turn right for 'Clitheroe, A680'. In 50 metres we go under the railway bridge then up a steady incline, thankfully leaving behind the worst traffic. Past Hyndburn Leisure (cycle shop) and straight on at the lights, then past The Grey Horse. Straight on at the mini-roundabout , now gently downhill, passing the sign to Accrington Stanley Football Club (so it really does exist!) and The Crown, leading into the Borough of Hyndburn.

At the lights we turn right along the B6321 – opposite is the Greyhound Inn. This is Whinney Hill Rd, which leads up steeply , no doubt causing the nags of past times to puff as much as I did! Past the enormous quarry we can look down on Accrington – interesting, if not particularly picturesque. Ahead is Great Hameldon. Down the 1-in-8 hill and past the industrial estate, now becoming Enfield Rd. Proceed uphill, over the level crossing at Huncoat Station, and up again past The Railway, followed by the post office and fish and chip shop. Here, amusing cycle lanes extend in a series of 20-metre lanes – better than nought! Follow the sweep of the road right, ignoring straight on, and steadily rising along Lowergate Rd. Under the pylons and past the Black Bull. Just before the White Lion, we turn left, following the sign 'Mill Hill picnic site, ¾ml' along our outward route, and thence back to the start. A worthy effort!

Summary

a) – b)
TL out of car park, over the A56(T), to T-jn
TL, past White Lion and Griffin's Head
TL along Burnley Rd
SO at first roundabout
Last exit at second roundabout
Uphill, past quarry (BW) to unsurfaced track (A56 on R)
SO uphill, under pylons
SO (ignoring L to fm) past marker boulders
SO, over moor, down to 'triangular jn'

b) – c)
TL then TR, down to track past Higher Hey Fm
SO, parallel to A56
SO, over lane
TL along lane towards resr. bldgs.
TR after 50m, lane to track
keep R past fm & cottages
SO, 'Sherfin Nook', keep R at fork
SO, steep descent to jn
TR (Clough End Rd) for 100m to lights

c) – d)
SO at lights for 100m to T-jn (Brook St)
TR, over A56T
TR (Rising Bridge Rd)
R at jn (Roundhill Lane) to T-jn with main rd
TL (Manchester Rd)
SO past Hollands Pies factory & Bay Horse

d) – e)
TL down Hurstead St (NB Push – FP status)
TR at bottom, along 'concessionary BW' to Accrington

e) – a)
TR at BW end, (opp. Victoria Business Centre)
SO, past police stn, to T-jn (Spring Gdns., Nuttall St)
TL, past Mighty Muldoon's (Abbey St) – SP, A680
SO at lights (SP A680), past The Queens
SO (Eastgate)
SO at lights (SP Huncoat)
TR at lights (SP Clitheroe, A680)
SO past Hyndburn Leisure (bikes), Grey Horse, The Crown
TR at lights (B6231) by Greyhound Inn
SO, steeply up, past quarry
SO, down 1 in 8, (Whinney Hill Rd, then Enfield Rd)
SO over unmanned level crossing & The Railway
SO (Lowergate Rd), past Black Bull
TL at SP 'Mill Hill Picnic Site,¾', over A56T
TR into start.

Route 10 – Rawtenstall

Distance: 15 miles
Off-road: 49%
Height Gain: 1250ft
Time: 2½ – 3½ hours
Start/Finish: Unofficial car park, immediately N of Clowbridge Reservoir, off the A56, half a mile N of Dunnockshaw and 2 miles S of Burnley, at start of bridleway. GR 832 784
Maps: OS Landranger 103, Outdoor Leisure, 21
Rating: **
Grading: Difficult
Gradient: A

'I wish you could have been there on the hill summit.' D.H. Lawrence, December 1918.

Route Summary

If I had to describe my experience of this route in a single word, it could only be 'dramatic'. I don't mean desperate, but the ambience was, undeniably, dramatic. The weather, so remarkably benign for most of these routes, showed its other face for Rawtenstall. And the English countryside is inextricably a part of its weather. On my first attempt I ran out of time, trying it too late in the evening, and beat a hasty retreat, albeit in good order, back across the moors. The following week a thunderstorm that had threatened all day broke with gusto as I pedalled across the, now familiar, moors. But the storm abated at times, permitting truly Turneresque splashes of light – England's greatest painter would have loved it, atop Cribden Hill!

As I cheerfully dashed off the moors, the heavens opened again and their lights went out, leaving me to puff up the A56 back to the start, cocooned in a world of my own torchlights.

Whilst the road-work is minimal (but beware the A56!), the moorland tracks can be both tricky to follow and occasionally steep and slippery. *This route is not recommended for the inexperienced!*

Route Description

a) – b)
Go straight on through the wide area by the reservoir (which is suitable for parking), through the gate at the end and directly on to the moor after a second gate, marked with a blue bridleway arrow. Ignoring the track that runs right around the reservoir, strike uphill, following the line of the pylons.

Shortly past a board explaining that this was one of many packhorse trails linking the Ribble valley with Rochdale. Climb a steep rise on soft ground then pass the bridleway sign on a thin track over the rise towards the pylons. At the high point, after the gate, pass a small restored cross. Go straight on to a distinct clough by the pylon.

At the cleft is a meeting of several tracks, with only a single footpath arrow between them. Some care is needed to trace the bridleway – I managed it at the third attempt! Continue through the cleft, over the stream and up the rise on the main track. The crucial point is a right turn at the top of the bank, following the cleft downhill on its left bank. Note that although the main track temptingly continues, shortly reaching the farm and road, it only has footpath status. The bridleway, however, takes one right down the valley to within 100 metres of the next off-road – so is well worth the effort.

Continue down the small track and straight on through the gate marked by a sign 'Footpath Round the Houses' into an obvious walled track which is likely to be muddy. Go gently downhill for 100 metres, straight on through a metal gate and across the track. It's good going for 150 metres, straight on through the gate (footpath goes left here) and down a deep gully to another gate. Continue straight on, along the right of the field for 50 metres, then turn right and through a bridleway gate, following the signpost across the stream and up the slope. Continue straight on, along the right of the field, passing a cattle trough and following the gully over the rise and to a junction of tracks. The main track crosses here, but we head diagonally left, first by a left turn through the wooden gate, then immediately right

Rawtenstall (Moors above Newchurch)

through the metal gate. Follow the 'holloway' alongside the drystone wall, passing the telegraph pole. It's wet at first, but as it rises we lose the stream. Straight on and in 100 metres through the gate and up to a high point where we come to another track crossing. Turn left and down the deep gully – it's quite rough in the bottom but we soon pass a farm (no gates!) and reach a good track. Easily down, all the way past the stream and bungalows, to its end – Peers Clough Rd.

b) – c)

Turn right and go along the road for 100 metres, around the bend with the high wall on the right, atop which is the church of St Michael's, Lumb in Rossendale. Turn left here, before reaching the Hargreaves Arms, 50 metres further along the B6238. Immediately over the stream, following the cinder-surfaced track around to the right. Straight on at the fork (ignoring a left), and the initial rise takes us nicely above the houses that line the main road. Continue straight on, ignoring a left to Salisbury Farm, and go gently down on the fine, grassy track, through a gate and alongside the low wire fence. The route is easily followed along the good track, through four gates, the last one being wide but almost collapsed, shortly after some decrepit barns. We follow a fine, grassy track between drystone walls for 100 metres to another gate. Straight on, slightly down and through another gate in 200 metres. The track is obvious.

In another 150 metres we leave the track that bends right and down to the valley, instead going straight on, up through a 4ft-wide gate (Rossendale signpost). Proceed up the slightly muddy gully (avoidable on the right bank), and through another gate at the top, leading to easier going. Keeping alongside the wall, go across a track and gently down between walls. Straight on through yet another gate, leading to an excellent grassy track running down a deep gully. Finally, go up a rise and along the good track, past some buildings, fine views, and to a broader, stony track. At the farm this becomes metalled and descends steeply to a T-junction at the bottom.

c) – d)

Turn right and down the main road (B6238) to the valley bottom. Exiting Shawclough Rd, turn left along the main road and past The Roebuck. Turn right up the road called, remarkably, Bridleway and go past Wills St. YMC. Continue steadily uphill to the T-junction and turn right along Turnpike Rd. Several churches are grouped around here. Steeply uphill again, over the brow past The Boar's Head, and straight on for Rawtenstall. Beyond the valley the hills rise all around, and ahead is our main objective – Cribden Hill (1317ft). Now down past The Old House at Home to the traffic lights at the crossing of the A682, with The Ram's Head at the junction.

d) – e)

Straight on over the lights, up the steep rise and 100 metres to the first right

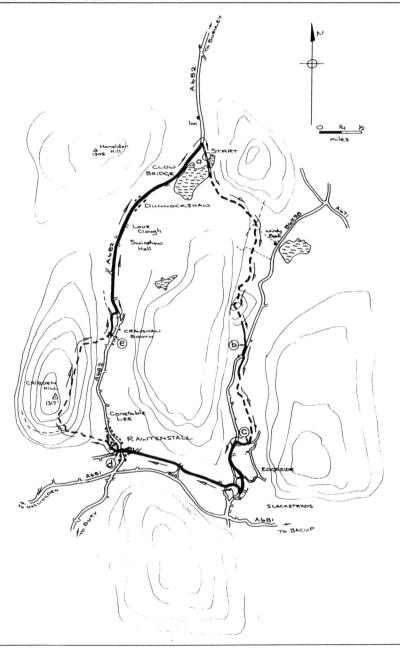

Route 10: Rawtenstall

turn. This is marked 'No Entry', so carefully push along the pavement here – otherwise access can only be gained from some way down the main road. Continue to the end of Whittle St., and the dog-leg takes us to Greenfield St. Take the first turn left, Beech St., for 100 metres to the start of the bridleway to Cribden Hill. We find this as a left turn opposite Prospect Rd, and follow the bridleway signpost up the clear track for the hill and its mast.

There's good riding up to the first gate, followed by a stony track between barbed wire fences going steeply up past the mast. Around a bend and up another rise to a prominent bridleway signpost, which indicates a right turn up the bank and through the gate to steep ground. We follow the sign (have faith!) and the bank proves negotiable with the option to carry or push, up a thin track that leads through the heather. Around the hillside it becomes, just about, rideable again. Through the narrow gate as we make for the farm, apparently at the top of the hill – now with magnificent views down the valleys. The undulating, narrow track expires as we approach the farm, and we continue over some steep, open grass. At the wall we keep to its left, and in 100 metres go through the gate and straight on between the drystone walls. Another 100 metres brings us to the farmhouse and into a small yard.

Across the metalled path and up the bank opposite to follow (still more faith!) the bridleway sign to the high-level track. In wet conditions this proved slippery, and negotiating the gate in good order was achieved more by luck than judgement. However, one is soon up (or not!) and on the good, well-marked track, making for the white post. Continue through a gate and slightly downhill in the gully, following the sign 'bridleway no.116'. Down the magnificent rocky gully, and through the metal gate to the next steep gully, bounded by stone walls. Exit through the farm, a little muddy but soon passed. A good, unmade track leads down – super riding! Go straight on, ignoring the bridleway on the right, and through the next farmyard – somewhat less muddy, being concreted. The lane, although unsurfaced, steadily improves as it nears the valley bottom. Through a gate and along the cinder surface to a T-junction , where we turn right down the semi-metalled lane. Keep right at the fork and then straight on, steeply down to the pleasant stream that flows along the valley behind the built-up area.

e) – a)

Ahead is the Mason's Arms. We turn left immediately after crossing the stream and follow it along the backs, past the industrial area. Turn right along Turton Hollow Rd, going steeply up, to meet the A682 a couple of miles north of Rawtenstall. Turn left along the Burnley Rd. All that remains now is to follow this road for a couple of miles back to the start. On the way we pass The Jester, continue the slow incline to The Glory and then reach 'Welcome to Burnley' sign. The sign to Dunnockshaw indicates that we haven't far to go, as the Clowbridge sign finally arrives. The incline is unrelenting until we reach the far side of the reservoir and can turn right off the road, back to the start at the beginning of the first bridleway.

Summary

a) – b)
SO into the BW, heading for the moors
SO uphill, rough track, parallel pylons
SO, BW arrows to isolated stone cross
SO to clough, by pylons
TR, immed. after cleft
SO, down under pylons
SO, thro' three gates
TR (50m after last gate), following BW SP, across stream, uphill
SO to track jn; go diag, L, following slight gully, along wall
SO to high pt., track crossing
TL, down deep gully
SO, past fm, down good track to end (Peers Clough Rd)

b) – c)
TR at rd to St Michael's Church, 50m before Hargreaves Arms
TL opp. church, BW (no SO); keep R, SO up cinder track
SO, many gates, variety of tracks
SO, off main track, thro' 4ft gate, SP Rossendale
SO, 50m muddy cleft, & continue
SO, steeply down to T-jn
TR (Shawclough Rd)
TL along main rd

c) – d)
TR ('Bridleway' – rd!), past Wills YMC, uphill
TR (Turnpike Rd), steeply uphill
SO, past Boar's Head, The Old House at Home
SO, across traffic lights (A682 crosses)

d) – e)
SO steep uphill for 100m
TR (NB push!) into 'No Entry' (Whittle St)
SO – dog-leg (Greenfield St)
TL (Beech St) for 100m
TL into BW (SP) – opposite Prospect Rd
SO towards pylon & BW jn; TR at SP, narrow track, bear L & between walls to fm
SO across yard to BW SP, opposite bank
SO (diag., following BW SP)
SO past white markers, to SP 'BW no.116'
SO downhill past two fms
SO, cinder track to T-jn (tracks); TR
keep R at fork to back rd – opp. Mason's Arms

e) – a)
TL, alongside stream
TR, uphill (Turton Hollow Rd)
TL along A682 (Burnley Rd)
SO past The Jester and The Glory to Clowbridge
TR, immed. after resr. to start.

Route 11 — Worsthorne

Distance: 21 miles (first loop – 13 miles)
Off-road: 36%
Height Gain: 1900ft (first loop – 1400ft)
Time: 3 – 4 hours (first loop – 2 to 2½ hours)
Start/Finish: Car park and picnic site, Hurstwood, nr. Worsthorne. GR 883 313
Maps: OS Landranger 103, Outdoor Leisure 21
Rating: *
Grading: Moderate
Gradient: B

'Yet the landscape is as much a man-made artefact as a natural one, and if we do not appreciate the transition from the industrial era to what we might christen the 'green age', we will all too easily misinterpret the world in which we live today.' Richard Hodges, *Wall to Wall History*, 1991.

Route Summary

The rural village of Worsthorne sits at the edge of Lancashire betwixt urban Burnley and Hebden Bridge, in the West Riding of Yorkshire. But between these we have a superb bridleway, surely one of the classic trails of the Central Pennines. It provides a great introduction to these high moorland crossings, and given reasonable weather should be accessible, even for the less experienced.

The return road is quite strenuous, but traverses attractive countryside, again with evidence of early mineral working in remote places. As I toiled up one steep hill, a couple of 'bull-nose' Morrises chugged down – evoking a perfect period scene for the 1920s onwards.

An optional second loop visits the grand Townley Hall and its park, home of a foremost Lancashire line, and now easily accessible from the town. Recommended less for the riding than the historical interest, it completes a fairly long but satisfyingly varied outing.

Route Description

a) – b)

An unobtrusive place to park in the village of Worsthorne may not be too easy to find, but an excellent alternative is the picnic site at the hamlet of Hurstwood. There is also the mainline station in nearby Burnley. Setting off from Hurstwood, we simply follow the road back to the T-junction and turn right. Cycle along for a few hundred metres and we come to the middle of Worsthorne. From the village centre the bridleway is easily spotted, run-

Worsthorne (Widdop Moor)

ning due east from the track opposite the Crooked Billet and alongside the fine parish church. The metalled lane soon leaves the few houses and the vicarage to begin its steady rise, its surface beginning to lose consistency as it passes the allotments. Pendle is already visible on the left. The track runs dead straight towards the pylons, and disappears over the hill beyond. After half a mile the tarmac is replaced by gravel. We continue between drystone walls, the local gritstone being much in evidence in walls and older buildings. Straightforward riding all the way up to the gate, which provides a handy excuse for a breather as the view now includes the reservoir down on the right, and a multitude of grassed-over mounds, evidence of the mineral workings of an earlier age.

The fine track is followed without difficulty as it undulates and winds around, but always heading eastwards. Straight on past the right turn for Gorple and Black Reservoir. Eventually, up the final rise to the crossing of tracks and signpost marked 'Worsthorne' and 'Widdop', 'public bridleway'. We continue straight on, beginning the long descent to the reservoir, although it is not yet in sight. Along the very enjoyable track until a surprise view suddenly reveals Widdop Reservoir, at the foot of a quick descent via a zigzag path. Following the track down to the reservoir, we go around to the right, along to the causeway to the road. Looking back, we see the impressive gritstone buttresses that guard the hillside above the reservoir.

b) – c)

Through the gate and turn left, soon beginning the climb on the pleasant, unedged lane. A rather fine ascent gains a downhill, enjoyable going on a bike! Go straight on at the fork, over a cattle grid and to the bottom. Climb the steep hill to a junction, where we turn left, past Stephen Hey Farm – where I passed a school party camped on an improbably sloping field – and finally up to a T-junction. Exiting Ridehalgh Lane, we turn left and go on to the crossroad. Straight on, following the sign 'Burnley, 3¾'. To the right is Colne, our next route, and further on is Pendle, reached a little later.

Descend the hill into Briercliffe, following the winding road as it climbs out of the village up Halifax Road to the crossroads, and the Sun Inn. Turn left along the Todmorden road. Past the Hare and Hounds and steeply down the undulating road ('single track road' sign), then uphill past the fine cottages sporting 'Briercliffe Society Award'. I was fortunate to enjoy some delicious blackberries from the hedgerow – one of the delights of 'cycling' uphill! Follow the road right (ignoring Shay Lane, straight on), travelling back to Worsthorne on this most delightful road. I was fortunate, as the evening light created an ethereal view down the valley towards Burnley. We arrive in Worsthorne from Extwistle Road, going past the Crooked Billet. Straight on through the village, past the village stores and the Ba Horse, along Omerod Street. Pass lush fields, all around on the way to the return to Hurstwood.

a) – d)

Continuing on the second loop, this is now Salterford Lane. Pleasantly down, then uphill to the T-junction at the top, where we turn right, following the sign 'Burnley, 2 ¼'. Then it's down again, past The Hollins, to turn left into Springwood Road (sign indicates that it leads to Applecross Drive and Deerpark Road). At the second turn left, we follow the 'brown temple' stately-home symbol for Townley Hall. Turn right at the T-junction, going quickly down past the golf course towards the (unseen) hall. At the crossroads we turn right (ahead is 'No Through Road'), and gently down to the bottom of the valley. Playing fields all around are still framed by a distant Pendle. Around the bends, ignoring the first turn left to the car park, then turn left along a short diversion to the hall. On the evening of my trip *A Midsummer Night's Dream* was, appropriately, being staged in the grounds. Returning from the hall suitably refreshed, we retrace our tracks and continue straight on, shortly arriving at the park gates – with the surprise that we are in the middle of Burnley!

d) – a)

Turn right along the road and straight on to the mini-roundabout. Continue straight on through the traffic lights, past the schools and the fish and chip shop, to the next lights, at The Wellington. Turn right for Worsthorne, along Brunshaw Road, shortly going past Burnley Football Stadium. A steady climb out of Burnley takes us past the exit for the away supporters, to a flat and straight stretch to the mini-roundabout. Turn left, following the sign to Worsthorne. Along Browside Road, we climb past Pike Hill Post Office and the Thornton Arms, then ride on interminably, still gaining height, to finally reach Worsthorne. A good spot to pause awhile before the easy run back (as earlier) to Hurstwood.

Route 11: Worsthorne

Summary

a) – b)
Hurstwood Picnic Site, SO to T-jn
TR to Worsthorne
SO in village, to church, before Crooked Billet
TR ('Gorple' SP)
SO, BW over moors to Widdop
SO (ignoring R to Gorple Ruin)
SO at BW crossing (Widdop Resr.)
SO around Resr. to rd

b) – c)
TL along rd
SO at fork, uphill (steep!) to T-jn
TL (Ridehalgh Lane) to T-jn
TL to Xrds
SO (SP Burnley 3¾)
SO thro' Briercliffe to Xrds at Sun Inn
TL (Halifax Rd)
SO past Hare & Hounds
bear R (ignore SO – Shay Lane), SP 'Worsthorne'
SO (Extwistle Rd), past Crooked Billet in Worsthorne

c) – a)
SO, thro' village, past stores, Ba House, (Omerod St)

a) – d)
SO past Hurstwood (Saltersford Lane) to T-jn
TR (SP Burnley 2¼)
SO past The Hollins
TL into Springwood Rd
2nd TL (SP Townley Hall – symbol)
SO past golf course to Xrds
TR past playing fields
TL (after car park) to Townley Hall & return

e) – a)
SO to Burnley at T-jn
TR
SO at mini-roundabout
SO at lights, past chip shop
TR at lights, (Bradshaw Rd), past The Wellington
SO, long uphill, past Burnley F.C.
SO to mini-roundabout, TL (SP Worsthorne)
SO along Browside Rd, past Thornton Arms
TR in Worsthorne (as before)
TL to Hurstwood (ditto).

Route 12 – Wycoller

Distance: 12 miles
Off-road: 42%
Height Gain: 1250ft
Time: 2½ – 3½ hours
Start/Finish: Wycoller Country Park, Trawden Road car park. GR 925 394
Maps: OS Landranger 103, Explorer 19
Rating: *
Grading: Moderate
Gradient: B

'Those healthful sports that graced the peaceful scene,
Lived in each look, and brightened all the green,
These far departing seek a kinder shore,
And rural mirth and manners are no more.'
Oliver Goldsmith, The Deserted Village, 1770

Route Summary

Wycoller, described elsewhere, easily justifies a visit in its own right. The route is not too long or taxing, compared to other routes in Lancashire – and a visit to the village nicely compliments the ride. It may, however, be busy in season, when a ride on the hills soon leaves the throngs behind. A tempting alternative for a longer ride is to combine this with the previous route, taking in the two classic bridleways of the area – Bouldsworth Hill and Widdop Moor.

Wycoller rests its reputation on the single, long bridleway that skirts Boulsworth Hill, following the old packhorse trail. This is a fine ride without excessive difficulty or effort, although it may have some muddy patches, but for the well-prepared it is a route for all seasons. The roadwork is quite enjoyable, demanding a fair effort as it gains height from the bottom of the valley at Colne, but the views are worth the effort.

Route Description

a) – b)

From the splendid car park, discreetly enclosed with hedges, we turn left and head back along the narrow lane to begin the route – assuming that the delights of Wycoller are best enjoyed after, rather than before the ride. At the T-junction turn right, go on for 200 metres and turn right, following the sign 'Laneshaw Bridge 1, Haworth 8¼, Keighly 10½'. Continue over the rise

Wycoller (Boulesworth Hill)

and pleasantly down to the T-junction by the stream, on the outskirts of
Colne. Turn right and follow the winding road as it makes the long climb
along the Haworth Road. Cycle past the 'Wycoller Park – Haworth Road car
park', (which makes an excellent alternative starting point). Up steeply
again past the right turn (track) that leads around to Foster's Leap. Legend
has it that Foster was offered his freedom if he could make the awesome
leap across the rocks – which he duly managed on horseback, only to continue over the cliff to their doom. We continue uphill, and in half a mile
cross the summit at the Herder's Inn, originating from the cattle-droving
routes that passed this way. Onwards, more easily now, for three-quarters
of a mile and, at the sweeping left bend we turn right into one of the region's
great bridleways – the crossing of Bouldsworth Hill on the old packhorse
trail. This was only recently restored to full bridleway status – hooray!

b) – c)

The track, although obvious, has a signpost but no sign. It passes through a
wide gate, then down on a good surface. This first part - to the path from
Wycoller – is now designated a BOAT (By-Way Open to All Traffic).
Straight on, past the sign to the Brontë Way. It joins from Wycoller, directly
up the valley, but only with footpath status. There's evidence in the grassy
mounds of the old workings – mostly limestone 'hushings' hereabouts. Not
far after the turn to Parson Lee Farm, we need to follow the right wall as the

main track continues straight on through a gate and into a dead end at Brink Ends Farm. Surprisingly, the right fork is not marked, but we go through a gate in the right corner of wall. Soon past a sign for 'Wyc' – not, I fancy, the Saxon name for the hamlet, just the elements disposing of the 'oller'! The track is generally in good condition, but there are some muddy patches, especially in wet conditions – although nothing that can't be overcome quite

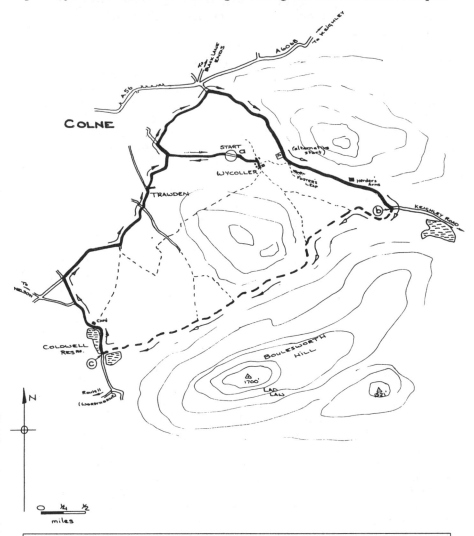

Route 12: Wycoller

easily with a modicum of cunning or effort. Continue past the isolated farm buildings, now with excellent views over the 'Forest' of Trawden – long since deforested by medieval kings.

Occasionally the old packhorse stones are revealed, and provide a good riding surface. Otherwise it's mixed riding: fording a small stream at one point, then over the hill and down to meet a metalled surface, where the Water Board have 'improved' the track on the way to one of their stations. We continue straight on, following the Pendle Way sign (witches symbol). Downhill on tarmac, uphill on concrete, then tarmac again as the road undulates and leads through a couple of gates. We then lose the metalled lane and are back on more appropriate stony, grassy or even muddy surfaces. Cross the occasional little stream and finally climb for the last time to high ground, where we can see the Coldwell Reservoirs ahead – along fine tracks. A footpath goes right to Coldwell, but we continue straight on the good track (only recently restored to bridleway status), and enjoy a pleasant ride down to the right of the reservoir. Through a couple of bridleway gates and out to the road.

c) – d)

Turn right and shortly go past the Activity Centre, which also has a café. Straight on up the stiff climb to the crossroads ('Colne 2, Nelson and Trawden'). We turn right towards Trawden, running merrily downhill on the Burnley road to the T-junction in the town. Turn right and then turn left at the next junction in only 20 metres. Downhill again, along Church St., then past The Rock (pub). Immediately after the war memorial we turn right (no signs), and pass The Old Rock (flowers) to begin a steep pull up to the high ground above Trawden. At the top are Trawden playing fields, where faint traces of the old strip-field system can be seen on the pitches – once arable ground for the villagers.

At the fork we turn right, following the sign 'Wycoller Country Park, ½'. This is high ground that gives a good view of Boulesworth Hill as we go past more of the innumerable footpaths – this area must have more footpaths than most other parts of England! The lane leads us directly back to the car park, but now we can continue straight on and into the hamlet of Wycoller. Directly ahead, on the skyline, can be seen the Huntsman's Leap that we passed earlier. Down at the centre of Wycoller we can pause for refreshments at the cottage café and stroll across the 17th-century packhorse bridge, or ford the slippery beck by the bridge. Across are the ruins of Wycoller Hall, and behind is the restored Aisled Barn, now an interesting visitor centre. Follow the beck up the valley and several fascinating bridges can be seen: from the supported gritstone slabs of the Clapper Bridge to the truly ancient Clam – a bridge formed by a single huge plinth of gritstone (now glued together after being swept away in flash floods!).

Summary

a) – b)
TL out of Wycoller Country Park, Trawden Road car park, Trawden Rd, to T-jn
TR, on for 200m to T-jn
TR (SP 'Laneshaw Br., Haworth, Keighley')
SO, downhill to stream & T-jn
TR, steep, long hill (Haworth Rd)
SO past Wycoller car park, Haworth Rd)
SO over summit at Herder's Inn, on for ¾ml

b) – c)
TR into BW (post only!) – good track (BOAT)
SO along long BW around Boulsworth Hill (Pendle Way)
SO, part metalled, to track to hill top
SO down to Coldwell Resr. to rd

c) – a)
TR, cont. past Activity Centre
SO to Xrds
TR (SP 'Colne 2, Nelson') on Burnley Rd
SO to T-jn in Trawden
TR, along 20m
TL (Church St)
SO, past The Rock
TR immed. past war memorial (no SP)
SO, steep uphill, past playing fields at top, to fork
TR (SP 'Wycoller Country Park ½')
SO to car park before Wycoller.

The Ribble Valley

Nowhere in Lancashire is there greater historical interest than the Ribble Valley. We begin at Whalley, now preserved from the marauding motors with a by-pass that has left town, Nab and river in relative peace. Before Henry VIII began his plunder of the kingdom, Whalley was the centre of control over lands that stretched through the Forest of Bowland and into each of the regions that we visit in Lancashire, bar those north of the Lune. Following the Pilgrimage of Grace in 1537, when the northern ecclesiastics protested about the king's incursion into their affairs, Whalley was implicated and the abbot finally paid for his devotion on the gallows at Lancaster Castle. All to no avail, and the abbey was destroyed along with nearby Sawley and numerous others, to feed the king's insatiable need for power and funds. Today the ruins are set in lovingly tended gardens, and the surrounding stone buildings form, once again, an important religious centre. Now it also welcomes visitors, providing a café in the old stables, overlooking the cobbled courtyard and ruins. The adjacent church has survived, complete with its rare Saxon crosses in the churchyard.

Invariably, there is something of interest in all the local villages, from the lonely ruins of Sawley Abbey, standing in fields overlooked by Pendle, to the unspoilt Waddington and Bolton-by-Bowland. Dotted around this fertile valley are some fine examples of Tudor and Jacobean country houses – none more impressive than Stoneyhurst College in Hurst Green, (just off the Ribchester route). Originating from the Shireburn manor of 1523, it has become famous as a foremost Catholic school, numbering amongst its old boys, J.R.R. Tolkien and Sir Arthur Conan Doyle. The supposed inspiration for *The Hound of the Baskervilles*, its castellated façade and dreaming spires face a vast lake and it retains treasures like the cope of Henry II, but can only be explored occasionally in the summer holiday.

Pride of place goes to Ribchester, a town with genuine Roman origins. Set beside the Ribble, it has a small museum and the outline of Roman baths. Founded by Julius Agricola in AD79 as one of the largest forts, it covered nearly 2¼ hectares (6 acres). Accommodating 500 cavalrymen, it was an important staging post between Chester and the northernmost outposts of the empire. In 1796 a magnificent bronze ceremonial helmet was found by a local boy, and resides in the British Museum, with a replica at Ribchester's museum. The wide and treacherous waters of the Ribble have been crossed, since at least Roman times, by a ford. Many accidents occurred, including the loss of Ribchester's first rector, Drago, in the 13th century, before the present stone bridge of 1774. The Whalley route reaches its southern banks, whilst the Ribchester outing follows on its north.

Enjoy the rides (noting the cautions further up the valley) purely for their intrinsic value or simply to explore the Ribble Valley – a bike again proving ideal for getting around its towns, villages and countryside.

Route 13 – Ribchester

Distance: 17 miles
Off-road: 59%
Height Gain: 700ft
Time: 2½ – 3½ hours
Start/Finish: Car park, near museum, Ribchester. GR 649 351
Maps: OS Landranger 103, Explorer 19
Rating: *
Grading: Difficult
Gradient: B

'It is written on a wall in Rome,
Ribchester is as rich as any town in Christendom'   Anon, Roman period

Route Summary

Ribchester is famous for its Roman associations, and must have been an important site in the link between the great Roman centres of Chester and Manchester with the Empire's northern outposts, in the Lake District and Hadrian's Wall. An interesting town, its situation on the bank of the Ribble, surrounded by rich agricultural land, provides the essence of the route.

Best done in dry conditions, this potentially muddy route provides bridleways that often require a push across rough pastureland. Although the height gain and gradients are less than for many other routes, the effort is relatively high. Route-finding alone renders this route in the 'Difficult' class. A portent of things to come further up the Ribble Valley, where I often found waymarking to be of a lower standard than elsewhere – and in places non-existent. Experience in map-reading and route-finding is a prerequisite here, as it is (even more so!) for Sawley and Bolton-by-Bowland.

Despite the drawbacks, these routes in the Ribble Valley have a singular charm, not unlike the West Country – but allow plenty of time and patience for route-finding!

Route Description

a) – b)

Turn left out of the car park, past the toilets and to a T-junction in 50 metres. Turn right and go along the main street, past the White Bull on the left. Its weather-worn pillars, supporting the porch, are reputedly from the Roman fort. When I rode here on a sultry evening in July, the annual (classical) music festival was being staged. Musicians in evening dress, strolling

THE WHITE BULL · RIBCHESTER

The White Bull, Ribchester

by the Roman Museum, fitted the scene perfectly. Follow the lane to the museum, ignoring a left to the Roman Baths remains, by a right turn; then bear left past the church and along the bridleway by the river. Go straight on through Lower Alston Farm, along a semi-metalled lane.

Follow the track (no signs so far) as it swings away from the Ribble and through a gate – where we meet the 'wavy-line' Ribble Way symbol. Back again by the river, continue on the flat through a field and straight on at a gate in 100 metres. Climb and go straight on through the next gate after 150 metres. Delightful riding as we pass through a small wood on a thin, winding track that emerges and runs down across the field to meet a broad, stony track from the right. We continue straight on down the track and through a gate, past the impressive Hothersall Hall, and then steeply up the concrete lane, leaving the river behind.

b) – c)

Over the rise the lane becomes tarmac as we pass Bashall's Farm and then turn left into the signposted bridleway. Along the metalled track, over speed bumps (on a bridleway!), over the cattle grid in 50 metres and then another. At the farm go straight on. On my visit the gates were only just hanging on, the helpful farmer explaining that his cattle had recently been stampeded through them – it's easy to forget the rigours of this way of life until confronted by a herd awaiting their evening milking. It was with some relief that I entered the empty field! We have to traverse the grassy field, devoid of any track or sign, on a diagonally-right bearing to pick up the right of the two slight gullies on the far side of the field. Again with some relief, we find a small gate almost hidden in the undergrowth at the gully, through which we pass, some 50 metres from the far left corner of the field. Down the tricky little track and straight on through a gate in 75 metres. Continue to an opening, bearing right and up the hillock, keeping by the left side of

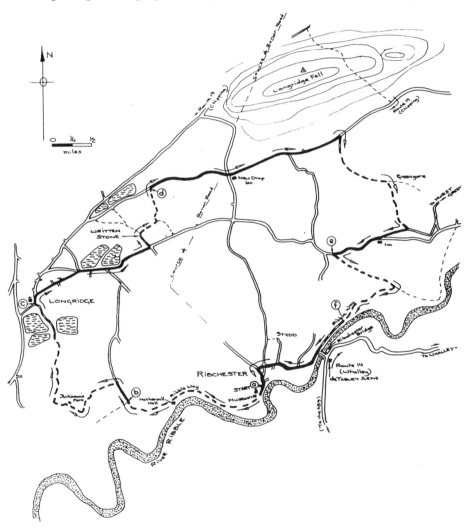

Route 13: Ribchester

the field. A 100 metre push finds a line of small, gritstone markers leading up to a gate. Over the rise, through gates and along a bumpy, enclosed track to a gate in 100 metres. Emerge by the house on a larger track.

Leaving Jenkinson's Farm House, we go straight on along the metalled lane. Turn right after the farm sign, along a concrete lane across high ground, with an open aspect open. Turn left immediately before the next farm, following the track and the 'footpath' painted on the wall (although this is still bridleway). Go straight on, through the gate and massive stone posts. Ride along the edge of the field and straight on through the next farm and several gates. We follow the lane as it makes a left turn, just before Bury's Farm. Fork right, still on a good, stony track and keep around to the left, by the wall. Proceed up to the semi-metalled lane, past Lamplighter's Cottage, and up the rise to the T-junction at the church.

c) – d)
Leaving the bridleway, we turn right along the road (B6423), and also right at the fork, still on the B6423. Heading pleasantly out of town, the long straight road leads past Alston Lodge, to the T-junction with the major road (care). Turn right to go past the reservoir and The Corporation Arms, then left into Lower Road – signposted 'Clitheroe 9, Whalley 8¾'. The straight road runs down then up a rise to a cottage where we turn left, following the bridleway sign 'Cottam House Farm'. Up the metalled lane to a crossing at the 'Written Stone', inscribed 1655. Turn right, following the metalled track to Cottam House, then turn left at the end of the farm (signpost – 'campsite'). Continue through the wide gate, past 'hut no.4', on the semi-metalled track and turn right at the gate, then left up the hill. Turn left, following another spurious 'footpath' sign up bumpy ground, just to the right of a (sometimes dried-up) stream, and a line of bushes. Continue uphill to a gate, inscribed 'horses please walk', and straight on to another gate in 30 metres, following a line of trees straight on. We continue up, about 80 metres from the left side of the field, finally emerging at a gate to the road, with a bridleway sign confirming our line.

d) – e)
Turn right along the road and on to the crossroads, having passed the line of the Roman road from Ribchester – now almost vanished. It's not even a footpath, just a holloway and a line on the map. The crossroads is marked by The Newdrop Inn. We continue straight on, following the sign 'Clitheroe 8, Whalley 7', (the Chipping route also visits this crossroads – in case a stop cannot be made this time). This continues as The Old Clitheroe Road as we reach a high point and are afforded great views across the Ribble Valley. On the left is heather and moorland, whilst on the right is grass and pastureland all the way down to the river. Past Huntingdon Hall Lane and shortly after the lay-by, as the road begins to descend, we turn right into the bridleway, following the sign down the tarmac track.

The semi-metalled track runs easily down through the trees, and straight on to the farm. Through the gate and straight on along a dirt track, coasting down through another gate, on a pleasant gravel track. Continue straight on at a bridleway gate to a grassy track, reminiscent of the Derbyshire Dales. It's excellent riding down to a stone cottage – Greengore – and out to the semi-metalled lane, following it down all the way and past New House to the T-junction with the road. Note that we passed an unmarked bridleway exit on the way down – a possible alternative. Turn right along the road (exiting Shire House Lane), going immediately past The Punch Bowl and continuing downhill. Past the sign 'Dutton', and to 50 metres before the T-junction make an acute left turn, down the semi-metalled bridleway (signposted).

e) – f)

Take the left fork along the good track, past the farm and the sign 'Private Road', continuing delightfully down and over a cattle grid. Shortly after the next cattle grid comes the turning off the metalled track that requires an extremely keen eye to find – principally because there is no trace of a track, and the landowner has certainly made no effort to identify its whereabouts. We pass the cattle grid, continue around the bend to the left and along a short straight to a faint kink left. A few metres before the small pond on the left (shown on the 1:25 000 map), we turn right into the field through the double metal gates. On my visit these were roped together. The law allows one to pass an obstruction to a public Right of Way. We go diagonally right across the field, down to the lowest point to find (with luck!) a gate amongst trees – obviously visited by horses (with a good sense of direction?). Go straight on up the other side, following an occasional white-painted post. Continue up the slope to the fence on the far side of the field and bear right. Follow the fence rightwards, with occasional white markings, down to the edge of the field, where another bridleway gate leads diagonally past some more white posts in the final field. In 150 metres we go over the rise and drop down, bearing slightly left and passing to the right of some bushes. Fifty metres on is another marker line, leading down to the track that passes a muddy cleft and finally down to the farm. We can now see the Ribble again, and at the exit from Dewhurst House Farm is a sign 'Bridlepath and mountain bikes follow the white posts'. Fair enough!

f) – a)

Along the semi-metalled, flat track past the log-piles near the river, and easily to the road bridge where the bridleway terminates. Go straight on the road back to Ribchester, past the Milehouse Farm Restaurant. In a few minutes we go past The Ribchester Arms and Stydd Lane (with its almshouses), to The Black Bull and the T-junction. Turn left along Church Street, simply following the signs to the museum, and finally turn right at the car park sign to the start. And only 17 miles!

Summary

a) – b)
TL out of car park, along for 50m; TR, past White Bull
SO, lane to museum; bear L along BW to Lower Alston Fm
SO, following Ribble Way (BW)
SO, past Hothersall Hall, steeply up lane

b) – c)
SO, past Bashalls Fm to BW
TL into BW (SP); SO to fm
exit fm diagonally R, across unmarked field
SO thro' BW gate – at gully in trees; bear R & uphill, near L of field
SO past marker stones to track
SO past fm to sign 'Jenkinson's Fm Ho' at lane
TR, along concrete rd, open ground
SO past fm, (two); TL by Bury's Fm; fork R, past Resr., to semi-metalled lane
SO, past Lamplighter's Cottage to T-jn at church

c) – d)
TR, along B6423
TR at fork, along B6423; SO, past Alston Lodge to T-jn
TR (care), past Corporation Arms
TL into Lowther Rd (SP Clitheroe 9, Whalley 8¾)
TL into BW, SP 'Cottam Ho Fm' (lane), to T-jn
TR at Written Stone (1655), to Cottam Ho
TL at fm, SP 'campsite', past 'hut no. 4'
TR at gate (green arrows)
TL & uphill (SP 'footpath' – but is BW)
SO, up fields to gate at rd

d) – e)
TR, along rd to Xrds; SO at Newdrop Inn (Old Clitheroe Rd)
TR (acute), downhill, BW(SP)
SO past fm, good track, to Greengore
SO along main track past New Ho, to T-jn (Rd)
TR, past The Punch Bowl; SO, past sign 'Dutton' to BW

e) – f)
TL (acute) BW, SP; fork L, past fm
SO, past 'Private Rd' sign
SO, over 2 cattle grids
TR thro' double gate (unmarked, no track)
diagonally right to dip in far side of field, to gate
SO, following white markers; SO to track, across muddy dip
TL, markers (sparse) to Dewhurst Ho Fm & T-jn

f) – a)
TR, semi-metalled lane (Ribble Way) to BW exit at Ribchester Bridge
SO to Ribchester, past Ribchester Arms, Black Bull
TL (SP 'Roman Museum'), Church St
TR into rd to car park – start.

Route 14 – Whalley

Distance: 19 miles
Off-road: 21%
Height Gain: 1050ft
Time: 2½ – 3½ hours
Start/Finish: Car park / picnic site, off A671, opposite road to Whalley. GR 741 360
Maps: OS Landranger 103, Explorer 19
Rating: **
Grading: Difficult (-)
Gradient: A

'Wall to Wall History ...' Richard Hodges, 1991, *(from the story of Roystone Grange)*

Route Summary

A delightful, not too difficult route, of a different character to the others in the Ribble Valley: it sees the best aspects (like the interesting ride and great views from the Nab), without the awkward route-finding or muddy conditions along the valley. This is my choice for a two-star route of the area – not too easy, some stiff but short climbs, great countryside, long country lanes – perfect on a bike! And wrapped around it all is the historic ambience of Whalley, with easy access from a surprisingly civilised start.

The scene is set in the historic town of Whalley, and a visit to the ruined abbey and its remaining intact buildings evokes a sense of history, to be savoured after an invigorating ride. The steep but short bridleway up the Nab is colourful and leads to good lanes across high ground, and on to superb tracks around the reservoirs. Whilst the second half is predominantly on-road, the stiff climb up to the Top of Ramsgreave leads to pleasant riding down to the Ribble, along its banks and back through the valley, where one can appreciate the 'high' of the road-cyclist – just keep pedalling and stoking up the endorphins!

Route Description

a) – b)
Remarkably, we start from an excellent picnic site, safely shielded by trees and off the trunk road that leads down to the A59. We simply set off going straight on at the lights, allowing safe passage to the old (and quiet!) road that runs down into Whalley. On the way down we are afforded views left to the wooded crown of Whalley Nab. At the mini-roundabout in Whalley, we turn left – opposite is the Dog Inn, to the right the Swan, and left is Whal-

Whalley (View towards the Nab)

ley Arms. Go along towards the river, past a chip shop and the Toby Jug tea-shop – refreshment in Whalley is not exactly a problem! Leaving King Street, we cross the Calder on a bridge widened in 1913, hopefully for the last time. As the main road bends right, we continue straight on, up Moor Lane. On for 100 metres, steepening, until we can escape by a left turn up the attractive, enclosed bridleway (well signposted).

Route 14: Whalley

Straight on, between the stone walls, through the wood. It's rideable at first, but when the gradient overcomes one it is no hardship to push through such a fine path. At the track crossing we follow the bridleway sign, taking us right and up through a one-metre-wide, steep and soft track, where riding is certainly not an option, and to push /carry is to avoid damaging the soft and potentially muddy surface – which certainly justifies going up, rather than down. A short carry over the rocky surface brings us in 100 metres to flat going, providing good riding, straight on and past the farmhouse, then down through the farm. Proceed through the gate and straight on past another farm in 150 metres, then past picturesque cottages and onto the metalled lane.

b) – c)

Follow Dean Lane, keeping right at the white house, past fine views left, then steeply up past Woodhaven. Over the rise to the T-junction and turn left. On to the next junction in 200 metres and turn left, down past Moor End and then Wyngate. We continue down Shawcliffe Lane and turn right into the bridleway (no sign), a broad gravel track some 200 metres before the T-junction. Following the excellent flat track, we round the left bend to views of a distant Pendle. Nearer the reservoirs, and 150 metres before the gate, we turn right down a good cinder track that leads to the foot of the reservoir dam, to find the first bridleway sign for some time.

Straight on through the gate and then after 20 metres, at the second gate, turn right, following the line of trees and track away from the reservoir and gently uphill. This is a small diversion from the most direct route to follow the bridleway – no problem, pleasant going! Continue alongside the wire fence, pushing as the grass gets longer, to a marker post, its bridleway arrow indicating a left turn at the end of the fence and just before the copse. Go across the field, following a faint path to a gate in 200 metres. Keep straight ahead, then follow the track as it curves around to head alongside the far side of the reservoir – pleasant riding with model route-marking. Straight on, around a jink in the stone wall, to the main track, which crosses from the dam. We turn right and up the broad track for 100 metres to find a gate that leads left alongside the reservoir (signposted). Left through the gate to follow another excellent track between the reservoir and a small wood, enclosed with a stone wall. Made for a mountain bike! Continue straight on through the gate at the end of the wood, running out to more open ground with a less obvious track. We continue gently down, 25 metres left of the stone wall, and then head for the gate to the road. A fine ride!

c) – d)

Turn right along the road and head uphill to shortly make an acute left turn, heading down York Road. Go straight on to the T-junction and turn right on to the main road. Pass another reservoir on the left as we head down to the town in the distance. Head down into suburbia and straight on across the

A666 (traffic lights), from Parsonage Road, with the Rising Sun and the Bull's Head at the junction. Up the steep hill past the station, and the interestingly named terraces – 'Paris' being about as unlike its namesake as it is possible to be! Past the 'Isle of Man' and ever upwards, with no respite until, appropriately, we finally reach Top-of-Ramsgreave at the Spread Eagle. Turn right here, down (hooray!) Saccary Lane, heading downhill all the way to the crossing of the A59 (care!).

d) – e)

Across the A59 is the Royal Oak, to the right is Rose Cottage (B&B). We continue straight on, having exited from Shawley Lane, directly into the fine bridleway. The track runs alongside the pub, then straight on through a gate in 100 metres, and past the farm, keeping right at the fork. Follow the track through the gate and straight on at the next gate, then down between hedges and towards a house and a gate. Turn right, following the bridleway arrow to a fine, semi-metalled track which goes under the pylons and suddenly out to meet the road at the apex of a bend. Super!

e) – a)

Turn left and cycle along until the road leads downhill past the deTaberly Inn to the Ribchester Bridge. We turn right immediately before the bridge (the previous route returned on the other side of the river), and follow the delightful lane as it meanders alongside the Ribble, through pastoral scenes akin to Veteran Cycle Club runs in mid-Cheshire. Go up a knoll, past Marls Wood and down to the T-junction. Turn left, following the sign 'Brockhall Village ¾, Whalley 3½'. There are fine views of Pendle to the right. Go straight on to Old Langho, past the half-timbered Black Bull (est.1867) in a rather picturesque setting. Straight on, the road leading down towards the River Calder, and revealing the vast brick span of the Whalley Viaduct a couple of miles distant. We cross far above (gratefully!) the A59 as we approach Whalley from the west. Go past St Augustine's R.C. school at the T-junction, where we turn left. Now in Billington, we pass under the bridge and past the Judge Walmesley with views, from the other side, of the viaduct and beyond to Longridge Fell (we'll be there soon on the Chipping route!), and the Forest of Bowland.

An easy downhill glide and we're suddenly back to the bridge over the Calder, swinging left and into the town, where the bridleway to the Nab sets off. We can simply retrace our tracks with a right turn at the mini-roundabout, and a puff uphill all the way to the lights and across the A671 to the start. Better still, continue straight on at the mini-roundabout and follow the signs left to find the glorious arches, gatehouse, church (with its Saxon crosses), and then into the courtyard and around the abbey ruins. Whalley shared with Sawley (next route), a dissolution of its abbey, but not before the abbot perished in his vain attempt to stem the tide of Henry VIII's wanton asset stripping – vandalism on a truly cosmic scale!

Summary

a) – b)
SO, out of car park, across the A671 (lights)
SO downhill to Whalley to mini-roundabout
TL, by 3 pubs(!)
SO past teashop to Calder Bridge (King St)
TL, up Moor Rd (steep)
TL into BW (steep, part soft, carry); fork R, cont. BW

b) – c)
SO, past Whalley Banks Fm, to Dean Lne
SO, steeply up to T-jn
TL to T-jn in 200m
TL, down, past Moor End
SO, along Shawcliffe Lne
TR (200m before T-jn) into BW (no SP)
SO, flat track to resr.
TR, cinder track at head of resr.
SO, thro' gates
TR & follow BW up slope (small diversion)
TL at BW SP before copse, across field
SO, follow track back to far side of resr.
TR, follow main track uphill for 100m
TL thro' gate, track alongside resr.
SO, past wood; bear L to gate & rd

c) – d)
TR, uphill
TL, down York Rd
SO, past resr. – Parsonage Rd , to Xrds
SO, over A666 (lights) – Rising Sun & Bulls Hd
SO, past Stn., long uphill to Top of Ramsgreave
SO to Spread Eagle (Hgr. Ramsgreave Rd)
TR down Saccary Lane
SO to Showley Rd, to A59 at Royal Oak
SO across A59 into BW
SO along BW
keep R at fork
SO to end BW

e) – a)
TL to de Taberley Inn
TR immed. before Ribchester Bridge
SO, past Marls Wood to T-jn
TL (SP 'Brockhall village ¾, Whalley 3½')
SO, past Old Langho
SO, bridge over A59 to T-jn (RC school)
TL (Billington), under bridge
SO to Whalley, over Calder Bridge
TR at mini-roundabout
SO, over lights (A671) to start.

Route 15 – Sawley

Distance: 12 miles
Off-road: 36%
Height Gain: 550ft
Time: 2 – 3 hours
Start/Finish: Sawley, roadside parking in village, or (better) Bolton-by-Bowland, as next route. (Sawley, off A59, GR 775 465)
Maps: OS Landranger 103, Outdoor Leisure 41
Rating: -
Grading: Difficult
Gradient: B

'The nation that forgets its past, forfeits its future.' Chairman Mao, circa 1950

Route Summary

The only route in the book without a 'star' indicates clearly enough my rating – and it comes with a clear health warning! Why then, you may reasonably ask, is it described at all? In the first instance, whilst I would strongly recommend it as a route not to do, it is there and has some admirable qualities. It includes a lovely part of the Ribble and the ruins of Sawley Abbey. Whether obstruction to our legal Right of Way should be confronted is not for me to say, but I can only relate my own experiences for others to make a fair judgement. A good compromise might well be to traverse the tricky section entirely on foot, which should mean that the Ribble Way is also accessible (subject to the enquiry decision). If tackling the route as described, it is necessary to check with the ROW officer about its current status (see appendix), travelling not only hopefully, but very carefully!

A route, akin to sunshine after a week of rain, that makes one truly appreciative of all the others!

Route Description

a) – b)

Heading east, Sawley is easily reached by taking the first of two turnings left, a half-mile off the fast A59. As we approach the village, the ruins of the abbey stand right beside the road, and one can walk freely around them – quietly and unattended, with the field stretching across the valley to Pendle. If an unobtrusive parking spot cannot readily be found, it is better to continue the couple of miles by road, following the signs, to a start common with the next route at Bolton-by-Bowland.

Sawley (Abbey ruins, Pendle behind)

b) – c)

From Bolton-by-Bowland's delightful riverside car park, compete with information and toilets, we turn right and head uphill through this gem of a village. Past the church , green and primary school, then the Caravan Club site at Fooden Farm, to a rather stiff climb up the fine, wooded lane. At the top of the hill is a lay-by that would provide a useful parking place should the village be full, which is quite possible in season. Follow the road around right at the pillarbox, signposted 'Gisburn 2½'. The fine country lane winds its way on towards Gisburn, past the 'Forest of Bowland' sign and down the 14% hill to the picturesque crossing of the Ribble. On the other side lies the bridleway of our next route, which we pass by as we head steeply uphill, past another of the Bolton bridleways on the right, and going straight on past Deer House Farm. Another climb, and then it's an easy run down to Gisburn and the A59.

c) – d)

Turn left along the A59, following the sign to Skipton, then a grateful escape in 50 metres by a right turn, at the sign indicating the A682. Past the sign 'Nelson, 6½', up the rise to a right turn at the sign 'Westby Hill Farm', and along a gravel track for the farm (bridleway sign). Pendle can be seen away to the left as we go past the farm buildings and then take an immedi-

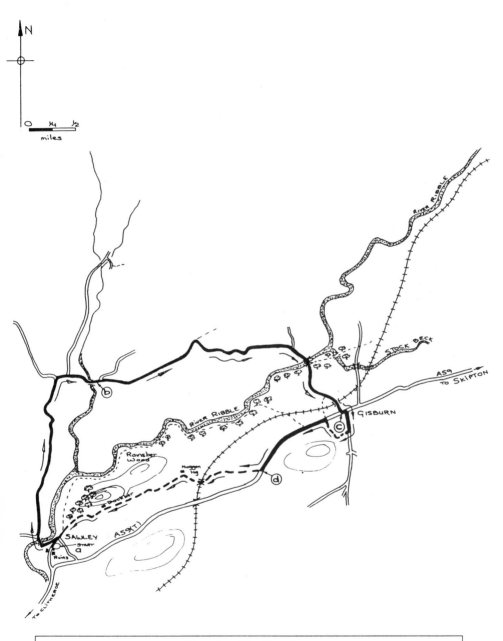

Route 15: Sawley

ate right turn along a drystone-walled lane, past the farmhouse. Continuing straight on, through a wooden gate in 20 metres, heading downhill across fine grassland. Although no track is evident, the line of the bridleway is followed by keeping near the hedge on the left, to reach the gate and bridleway sign at the A59.

Turn left along the A59 (care), following it past a bridleway sign and up the rise past the Stirk House Hotel on the right. Around the sweeping left bend, to a milepost and sign 'Skipton, 12'. Immediately after the house on the right and a some trees, we turn right into the field at the wide gate, following the wooden bridleway sign.

d) – a)

Now for the fun! The sign at the road provides a good start, indicating a diagonal line across the field, but beware for this is the last proper sign before we reach the end, and it would seem that the landowners are, shall we say, less then keen to promote the legal bridleway across these lands. Whilst they may be applying at the time of writing to have the bridleway downgraded, until a proper legal decision has been made right is on our side – but the current status should be confirmed before embarking on the route to ensure that it is still legally possible, as I met a farmer who was aware neither of his legal responsibilities nor common countryside courtesy.

Follow the line of the signpost diagonally across the flat, bumpy field to a gate through which we continue in the same line. Near the left corner and about 200 metres from the right-hand fence is a gate with a yellow footpath marker (still bridleway). We pass straight on across another field with no indication of a path, following the line of the three trees. Straight on through the metal gate at the last of the trees, now heading for the farm, across flat and bumpy pastureland. Continue straight on through the gate (I found it tied up) and across the next short field to the farm.

Go straight on through the farmyard, where I had to lift over a succession of three gates to reach the lane beyond. Along the unsurfaced lane past some fine old buildings to the small T-junction to turn right, going immediately over the railway bridge. Continue to the fork, then through the wide metal gate and diagonally across the field, following the footpath marker. Across the open field with the faintest of tracks, and up between a pair of hawthorn trees, pushing up the rise through long grass. Continue over the rise to the top left-hand corner of the field and the stile. Follow the footpath arrow (wrongly marked, yet again) over the stile (!), going left in the direction of the arrow and alongside the field edge for 200 metres to another fence on the right, where we can see the farmhouse. Over another stile and turn right towards the farm for 20 metres, then turn left. In another 20 metres we follow a line of trees through a wide metal gate and another erroneous footpath sign, straight on, with Pendle on our left. Following along the line of the fence and trees, we go over another stile, with barbed wire carelessly stapled across, and down to another gate, which required yet another lift. Now head diagonally to go through a gate in 100 metres. Turn left, following the line of the fence to reach a small, isolated wood.

Climb over the gate, jammed against rocks, and turn left, keeping to the right of the fence. Go around to the left, and all the way down to the bottom left-hand corner and over another difficult gate to the wood. We're finally at the nadir of the route. The bridleway is clearly mapped through the wood, but to reach it one has to precariously cross barbed wire and fight through the remnants of what was once the path, exiting with similar difficulty at the far side. Obviously it was not intended that one should pass this way, but to simply circumvent the wood takes us off the legal line, and there was no indication to this effect. So I pressed on, heading rightwards to the obvious gate about a quarter of a mile away, which marks the junction with the good track on to which we turn left and go down past the farm. It was here that I was astonished to be accosted by a farmer who wouldn't listen to reason, and I was left with no option but to press on quickly!

The dirt track continues as a semi-metalled lane, going gently downhill to the T-junction with the tarmac lane where we turn right. In 75 metres turn right again to Sawley Lodge, where we finally find a bridleway sign! Shortly down to the banks of the Ribble, and a left fork to Sawley ruins. Although I actually compounded the torture by continuing past Sawley House and along the Ribble Way, finally emerging further up the A59, this is the subject of an imminent ROW status decision and is hardly an appropriate route for a bridleway as it is potentially so muddy. Despite this, when resolved it would surely make a good walk, returning on foot along the route described above – thus avoiding confrontation with unreasonable landowners or misinformed farmers.

Summary

a) – b)

Past the Sawley ruins, heading N

TL, following SP 'Bolton-by-Bowland'

TR at pub, for B-by-B

TR at fork, for B-by-B

b) – c)

SO to B-by-B, over bridge and past car park

SO, up steep hill, past Fooden Fm (CC club site)

Follow rd and SP 'Gisburn 2½'

SO, sp 'Gisburn 1'

SO, down 14%, over Ribble, up hill

SO, past BWs, to Gisburn

c) – d)

TL at T-jn, along A59, (SP 'Skipton') for 5,0m

TR, (SP 'Nelson, A682')

SO, uphill

TR, (SP 'Westby Hill Fm')

SO, past fm, and downhill over grassland for ½ml to A59

TL, along A59, (care!)

SO, past Stirk Ho Hotel, milepost, SP 'Skipton 12', to BW SP

d) – a)

TR, following BW SP across open fields

—refer to text as route-finding problematical —

SO, past Dockber Fm, to semi-metalled lane and T-jn

TR, along for 75m to jn

TR, and down to Ribble

TL, follow rd back to start.

Route 16 – Bolton-by-Bowland

Distance: 18 miles
Off-road: 59%
Height Gain: 800ft
Time: $3\frac{1}{2}$ – $4\frac{1}{2}$ hours
Start/Finish: Bolton-by-Bowland, riverside car park. GR 784 494
Maps: OS Landranger 103, Leisure Series 41
Rating: *
Grading: Difficult (+)
Gradient: B

> 'Alone, alone, all, all alone,
> Alone on a wide, wide sea ...
> And never a saint took pity on
> My soul in agony.'
>> *Samuel Taylor Coleridge (1772 – 1834), The Ancient Mariner*

Route Summary

What a Jekyll and Hyde route! A delightful starting point at one of the region's most attractive villages leads to pleasant country lanes; brilliant first, last and penultimate bridleways; a unique crossing of the Ribble at Nappa; and the isolated hamlet of Paythorne and the Buck Inn. All this contrasts dramatically with bridleways which are among the most difficult to find or follow! Actually, I found almost all of the off-road terrain quite pleasant, given reasonable weather. No awful wheel-clogging clay (so common in the Midlands and South of England), but mostly the grass and rough pasture which are typical of the region, if atypical of Lancashire. But be prepared to exercise a high level of route-finding skill on the intermediate off-road sections, for marking is almost totally non-existent, apart from single signs at the roads, and very often the way leads across fields devoid of tracks. The high grading is a reflection of this route-finding difficulty, the actual riding being relatively undemanding – but it still requires a degree of tenacity to enjoy the outing.

An easy ride this is not, but for satisfaction in following almost obscure, ancient tracks, it takes some beating!

Route Description

a) -b)

From the car park in the delightful village, we turn right and follow the road uphill and along the winding and undulating country lane towards Gisburn, as described for the previous route. On reaching the bridge over the Ribble, however, we turn left on its far bank, into the well-marked bridleway. Along the metalled lane signed 'hospital' (turns out to be veterinary), and down the only way that isn't marked as private! Straight on, over the cattle grid, and past the great mansion on the left to continue ahead through a wide gate. At the unusual fork, we go straight on down the track that bisects the two arms of the fork. An excellent, enclosed track, this crosses the stream in 100 metres, goes past a house and up a fine, stony track that emerges from the woodland to run across open ground and pleasantly down to the road crossing. When I passed the wood was liberally filled with pheasants – a pleasant ride.

b) – c)

Go straight on across the road and into the field opening, following the bridleway sign across the open field. Bear right, crossing the stream at a natural bridge (no obvious track), and making directly for the bridge where we go under the railway, near the right-hand corner of the field. Having slipped carefully under the electric fence and through the muddy passage under the bridge, we turn left after 20 metre. Through the first gate, going diagonally across the fields, making for Painley Farm. A cattle track leads the way to the farm, and we continue straight on without too much difficulty until the crossing of the road is reached.

c) – d)

Turn right and follow the road past the first bridleway on the left, at Horton Green, and on to Horton. Here we turn left at the triangular green and ride along the obvious unsurfaced track that leads past the farm buildings and out to open ground. Over the cattle grid and left at the fork in the semi-metalled track as it winds down a dip and up the other side. Over the rise it runs easily past Yorsdale and then to the right of Lower Paradise Farm. Straight on through the gate, 50 metres after the farm. Along the stony track past the barn to the gate in 150 metres. Continue straight on for 150 metres along a much less distinct track, and through another gate to go across open ground, making for a telegraph pole on the far side of the field.

Once over the rise, the farm (Horton Pasture) comes into sight. Continue 50 metres to the left of the fence, going through an opening at the bottom of the field, and then heading up the faint path. Across the open field to the farm at the top of the rise. Proceed through an old stone gateway, under the electric fence and through the farmyard. Pass a gate and cattle grid and along a metalled track for 50 metres. Tricky enough to follow, this was just the softening-up for what is to come. Stamina and well-developed map-reading skills are vital – and even then the Ancient Mariner came flitting into my thoughts as I pondered the map. Plenty of time and a fine day are highly desirable – it was already later than planned and a once-brilliant sky

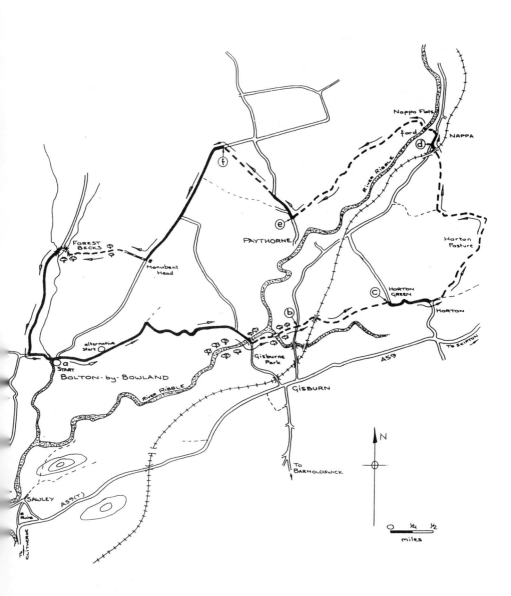

Route 16: Bolton-by-Bowland

was turning ever darker, making the subsequent successful escape all the sweeter.

After the farm, as the road curves right, we continue straight on along the faint track, hard by the fence on the left. Go up the slope and turn left through the first gate, then across the open field, over the knoll, past the enclosed plantation and down to the bottom right-hand corner. Exit through the gate in the drystone wall, with a right turn to follow alongside this wall as it heads away from the farm. Continue along a thin track, alongside the course of the stream, down to the right-hand field corner. Right through the gate (a bit wet here), and alongside the wall for a few metres. We now, daringly, strike diagonally left across the open field. It's a good push up through long grass in this isolated spot! Far away on the left is the reassuring shape of Pendle – but where are we? Continuing across the field we reach the fence on the far side. From halfway up the slope, we go left, down the slope, following the fence as it kinks back. Shortly – lo and behold, is a bridleway gate, although, as expected, without a sign.

Through the gate and curve around right past a few trees below the top of the hill. It's straight on through (over) the next wooden gate, which leads out to a small triangular 'green'. We turn right and along the walled track, which, although sadly neglected (little wonder as it has been so difficult to find), is clearly the way. Continue for 50 metres to another gate and then straight on between the bank and stone wall. Along the holloway and over the rise to reveal a view of the track running downhill. It continues as Needles Hall Lane according to the map. Straight on, going through two gates at 100-metre intervals and following, for once, the obvious track. Continue straight on, up the rise and through a gate in 150 metres. Earlier optimism about the fine track surface is found to be misplaced as we push through long grass, but at least the line is easily found by following the wall straight on. In half a mile we continue through a wide metal gate, (Cow Gate Lane on the map). Through an enclosed track and past old stone gateposts, to a rather fine track that runs downhill for 100 metres to a gate under the railway track. Finally to a last gate in 100 metres, and out to the road.

d) – e)

Turn right along the road (care!), and shortly down the slope, turning left at the sign 'Nappa... Manor House Farm.' This is the (unmarked) bridleway, a metalled lane which leads past the farm to a T-junction where we turn left. The bridleway runs gently down and across the grass in front of the cottages (with due respect) to suddenly meet the fast-flowing Ribble – an idyllic scene, until it's realised that we have to cross here, either by fording the river or hopping across the stepping 'stones'. These are actually concrete plinths. All is well (carrying the bike) until the middle, where the current has tipped over the steps – best crossed on a hot day! On to the far bank and (still unmarked), we go straight on through the nearest gate, and up through a clump of trees 50 metres ahead. Through a gate and straight on up the hill, ignoring the track that runs off left. Pushing up through the long grass on the right of the field, we follow the wire fence to the white house (Nappa Flats). Following the stone wall past the house, we continue straight on through the gate ahead, ignoring the track going right. Go straight on alongside the fence and through the gate, along the grassy lane going downhill – and pedalling for a change!

Through a gate in another 50 metres and up the rise on a dirt track, past the barn 200 metres to the left. Continue straight on along this good track and through a metal gate into a field, exiting through a gate near the right-hand side of the far wall. Continue straight on, past the great pile of tyres and farm on the left. The old track is edged by low, stone walls and submerged by the undergrowth so a push is required as we go along its bumpy bed. We continue straight on through a wide, metal gate, which actually has a white arrow pinned to its other side. Past a muddy section and on to a semi-metalled track to a junction, where we turn right and follow (oh, luxury!) a semi-metalled track past a farm and straight on, over a rise for about a mile. Once through the next farm and a scattering of houses, we reach civilisation again as the great run down reaches the T-junction in Paythorne. Here, at last, is a bridleway sign, pointing back! A rather faded information board does its best to extol the virtues of the Ribble valley, but perhaps of more immediate interest is the inviting Buck Inn across the road.

e) – f)

Turn right, along the road past the Buck Inn, and uphill past Twyn Ghyll caravan park to top the rise. At the apex of the bend to the right, we continue straight on through a wide gate, following the well-signposted bridleway. Continue straight on along the obvious track, ignoring a left exit, and through the first of a series of bridleway gates along a well-marked track – now this is more like it! A terrifically sinuous track offering absorbing (although not very quick) riding, up and down banks amongst the trees. Through a bridleway gate, signposted, and another, then along the left side of an open field. Continue through the avenue of trees, then back to riding up and down the banks and straight on through a bridleway gate. There's a little mud around, but nothing serious, as we go through another (unmarked) gate. Straight on along the right side of the open field, alongside the twin wire fences. Although flat, the bumpy pastureland makes for hard work on the last quarter mile, to the gate that leads into the trees. The road crossing is just beyond. Much better!

f) – a)

Turn left along the road, and past the faded Ribble Valley sign with, once again, glimpses of Pendle ahead. A pleasant lane, allowing recovery before the last sortie of the route (and day, I fancy!). Straight on past the left (to Gisburn, 2½), following 'Bolton, 2'. At Monubent Head Farm, we turn right into the well-marked Forest Becks bridleway. An entirely different proposition, this part is not to be missed! Pedalling along the broad, stony track I found particularly pleasant, with all the previous graft behind and a setting sun on the left. Gently down, past the farm, straight on through the gate along the obvious track, downhill all the way! Finally, the track is barred, so we execute a simple side-step right and continue with the original line of trees hard to the left, until we can rejoin the avenue as it rolls delectably down. Through a narrow gate, occasionally past innocuous muddy patches, to another gate in 200 metres. Follow the curve right as it dips down through ancient woodland to the gate at the bottom. The obvious track beyond leads past the hamlet of Forest Beck to the bridge over Monubent Beck, and our return road.

Go past the cottages and turn left at the road to follow it for the mile to the T-junction. Turn left and directly back to the start. Wow!

Bolton by Bowland (fording the Ribble at Nappa)

Summary

a) – b)
TR out of the car park, and uphill out of the village
SO, up steep hill, past Fooden Fm, (CC club site); Follow rd and SP 'Gisburn 2½'
SO, SP 'Gisburn 1'
SO, down 14%, over Ribble, to far side of bridge
TL, into BW, uphill, past mansion (Vet. hosp.)
SO at unusual 'Y' jn; Down enclosed track, across stream
SO, good track to rd

b) – c)
SO, across rd, into BW, open field; Diag. R across field and stream, under bridge
TL, 20m after bridge, diag. across field
SO, past fm to rd
TR, along rd to Horton (hamlet)

c) – d)
TL at triangular green, into BW (SP), for 50m
Fork L and SO along good track, worse later
SO, past Horton Pasture Fm
SO, past fm at top of rise; Bear L after fm, (unmarked), off main track
TL, across field (no track)
TR, alongside wall
TR, wall corner, on for 10m
TL, across open field, no sign, no track, all alone!
SO, thro BW gate; SO,thro fields, to triangular green
TR, follow walled track, long BW, variable conditions
SO, under railway, on for 100m, to rd

d) – e)
TR, along rd
TL, into BW (unmarked) at SP 'Nappa'; TL at fm
SO, past cottages, to Ribble
Ford, by stepping stones, SO up bank
Bear R (unmarked), SO to 'Nappa Flats'
SO, ill-defined, many fields, unmarked
SO, past England's Head Fm
SO, metalled track, to jn
TR to rd, T-jn at Paythorne
TR, past Buck Inn, uphill

e) – f)
SO at apex, into BW (SP); SO, along BW (good SPs), to exit at rd crossing

f) – a)
TL, along rd; SO, (SP 'B-by-B, 2')
SO to Monubent Fm and BW
TR into BW (SP 'Forest Becks, BW')
SO, along BW, good track, down to exit at fence
TR along short track, over bridge to T-jn (Forest Becks)
TL, along rd, 1ml to start.

Pendle

Barley is our first venue as we finally reach the hill which we have so often glimpsed from afar – and it proves well worth the wait! 'Barelegh' was the medieval name given to the village (which was formed as a 13th-century Vaccary) and means infertile meadow, or 'bare lea'. It has become the centre for a visit to the summit of Pendle 'Big End', at 1831ft an impressive contribution to Lancashire's finest hills. Perhaps not quite a Grindlewald to the Eiger Nordwand. Nevertheless, a charming place, providing a grand starting point for both of the region's routes. Combined, these provide one of the best in the itinerary. Whilst Barley's origins are firmly tied to agriculture, the tentacles of the Industrial Revolution even crept up here – with two mills being established in the 19th century. They have now been happily overtaken by the march of progress, but for a time provided much-needed supplementary income for hard-pressed land workers, and even today hill farming on marginal land is an economy on a knife-edge.

No visitor to Pendle can ignore the witches' folk-lore. Perhaps Pendle was only the focus for the most visible cases, for witchcraft, in one form or another, has been a normal facet of life down the ages. Superstitions are a link with this past – or don't you 'touch wood', walk around ladders, or cast a wary eye on Friday the 13th (like me)? Imagine the scope for witchcraft in the Middle Ages, in a closed world with rudimentary medicine, science and technology, against a powerful religious background; even Isaac Newton spent at least half his prodigious life in an ardent study of Alchemy!

The scene was set by King James I, not for nothing known as 'the wisest fool in Christendom'. The king's obsession with witchcraft meant that officials were inevitably predisposed to uncovering such practices. It only took a series of bizarre happenings in the villages surrounding Pendle, to bring the two warring families of the Demdykes and Chattox, headed by their decrepit, octogenarian matriarchs, to the Assizes in Lancaster Castle. Dragged down with them was Alice Nutter. A member of the 'landed classes', she had the misfortune to cross Roger Nowell, chief prosecutor for the crown, in a bitterly-fought land dispute. Likely, he took his revenge, and Alice's silence at the trial, probably to defend others of the persecuted Catholic faith, saw to her denouement. Of the nineteen committed to several months in the dungeons at the castle awaiting trial, ten were sentenced to the gallows, nine being from Pendle. Old Mother Demdyke expired before reaching the court, which is hardly surprising considering the appalling conditions. A conducted tour of the castle includes the opportunity to experience being locked up for one minute in the total blackness of the dungeon with a dozen others – leaving one with little desire to return to the 17th century! In August 1612, the legend of the 'Witches of Pendle' was cast, and leaves us as grimly fascinated as the tale of Guy Fawkes – so don't miss their little shop in Newchurch, or dally near Pendle on Hallowe'en!

Route 17 – Barley

Distance: 7½ miles
Off-road: 58%
Height Gain: 950ft
Time: 1½ – 2½ hours
Start/Finish: Barley car park & picnic site. GR 823 403
Maps: OS Landranger 103, Leisure Series 41
Rating: *** (when combined with Downham)
Grading: Difficult
Gradient: A

'... we came near a very great and high hill, called Pendle Hill, and was moved of the Lord to go
to the top of it ... and it was so very steep and high.'
George Fox, founder of the Quaker movement, 1652

Route Summary

A great route in its own right, but surely perfect as an hors-d'oeuvre to the
Downham route, which is how I did them on an ideal late summer's afternoon – providing the definitive 'three-star' outing, by finishing in the dark.

This is quite a short outing, giving plenty of time to explore the region,
including the delightful villages visited on the next route; for on a longer
expedition, like Downham, one often can't spare the time to explore at leisure places such as Sabden, Pendlestone and Newchurch. Whilst our route
only traverses beneath the summit of Pendle, it does follow a fairly quiet
way, avoiding the obvious path to Big End. However, leaving the bikes near
Pendleside Farm, a relatively easy (!) ascent can be made on foot to the summit, up the obvious track, providing even better views in fine weather. The
latter part of the bridleway around Pendle and the steep descent demand a
fair degree of skill. So, not recommended for the inexperienced – but the
difficulties are short and, given reasonable conditions, the epitome of hill-
riding. Excellent!

Route Description

a) – b)
From yet another excellent car park, we turn left and along the road towards Barrowfold, but only for 50 metres. Then we turn left into the clearly
marked bridleway that runs behind the car park. Go along the fine lane,
over the stream and past the delightful hamlet of Narrowgates, with its picturesque cottages clustering around the 19th-century mill, now converted

Barley

into desirable residences – for the Industrial Revolution managed to spawn two mills, even as deep in the country as Barley. For the Victorian entrepreneurs, where there was water power, there was a way for industry! The other mill was wrecked in the floods of 1880, and now forms the North West Water filter station (appropriately!) for the reservoirs which we pass on our return to the village.

From the track, to turn left at the sign 'Pendle footpath'. Follow a metalled lane past cottages, leading around to the right and then steeply uphill. Pass through a delightful wood and in 200 metres go past Whitehough Outdoor Education Centre. We turn right immediately after the centre, following a small track, and then turn left to following a burbling stream through captivating countryside – just about rideable, but what does it matter in such pleasant surroundings? At the head of the stream, past the holly bush and enclosed track, we come to a bridleway gate, from which we go straight on uphill to the next gate. Continue up the hillside, over open fields to the right of the wood for 200 metres. Next go over good, steep grassland to the bridleway gate in the drystone wall. We continue straight on (unmarked), heading over the steep rise and begin to ease right, along a faint track line, to run alongside a fence that approaches from the left. Another 50 metres and we reach the top of the hill, and follow the track straight on as another fence appears from the right, leading us over the crest. In 100 metres go

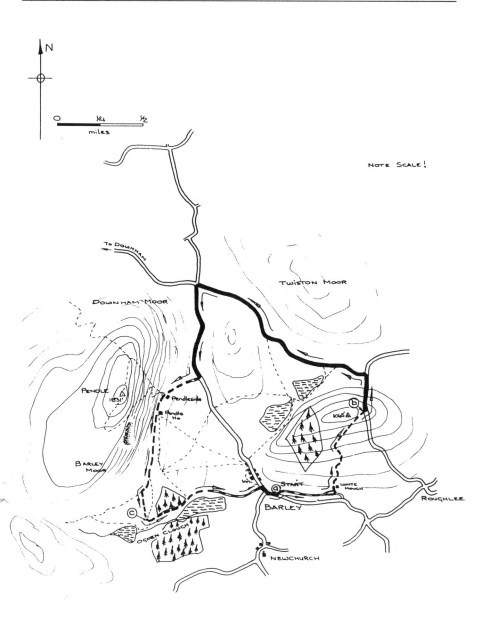

N

0 ¼ ½
miles

NOTE SCALE!

To DOWNHAM

TWISTON MOOR

DOWNHAM MOOR

PENDLE △ 1831'

Pendleside

Pendle Ho

BARLEY MOOR

1065 △

ⓑ

ⓒ

OGDEN CLOUGH

ⓐ START

BARLEY

WHITE HOUGH

ROUGHLEE

NEWCHURCH

Route 17: Barley

down to the gate and the road. Hardly surprising, the views are magnificent from here, an effort well-rewarded!

b) – c)

Turn left along the road, go up the rise to the T-junction and turn left (signpost pointing back – 'Roughlee 1¼'). Down towards the reservoir, and filling the frame ahead is Pendle, 'Big End'. Once over a couple of cattle grids on this unfenced lane, turn left at the crossroads, following the signpost 'Burnley 7, Barley 1½'. A long grind uphill finally leads over the top, and shortly after starting the descent we turn right into the obvious metalled track, following the prominent bridleway signpost directly to Pendle. Go straight on, over the cattle grid and right at the fork, with 'Pendle' painted on the rock. Head towards Pendleside Farm (1778), but turn right through a gate just before reaching it. Turn left immediately to run alongside the farm. We head towards Pendle House, with Pendle summit rearing up on our right.

Continue straight on alongside the fence, then drystone wall, passing the footpath return to Barley. Straight on through the gate, 20 metres up the moor and continue along the same line, following the interesting track across open ground - superlative views over Barley and the reservoirs. Pass through another gate as we traverse below Pendle. Past the isolated cottages below, and through a wide gate as we follow the track near the right fence. Follow the high ground around a tricky little cleft, where the track is in danger of vanishing into the gully. Go through the wide gate to a junction of tracks.

Ignoring the locked gate on the right, we turn left through the gateway (unmarked) and across the open field of short grassland, running alongside its left wall. Steadily downhill for 100 metres, then suddenly the reservoir is revealed below. We continue on the same line down the excitingly steep grass, making for the gate in the left corner of the walls – the last bit being a little tricky, and the stone walls at the bottom immensely solid!

c) – a)

Turn left along the excellent, crushed-stone track, heading down past the small wood on the left and the lower reservoir - now running easily along between drystone walls. These gritstone walls display the rusty tints indicative of the local ores. Pass the Filter House as this delightful riding suddenly brings us back into the middle of Barley, at the road.

Straight on across the road, following the sign for the picnic site, and we're back to the start. A fine outing!

Summary

a) – b)

TL out of the car park, SO for 50m

TL into BW, (SP)

SO, along track, past cottages

TL, SP 'Pendle'

SO, steeply uphill, on for 200m

Past Whitehough Outdoor Education Centre

TR, behind centre

TL, going uphill by stream

SO, up hill, across fields

Bear R, over top of hill, SO to rd

b) – c)

TL, along rd to jn

TL, along to Xrds

TL, (SP 'Barley 1½, Burnley 7')

SO, uphill, going over summit

TR into BW (SP and Pendleside Fm)

SO, along good tracks

Keep to R of fm, cont. SO along BW track

SO, around Pendle, across moors

SO, across cleft, bit tricky, to track jn

TL into open field (no SP)

SO, down steep field to bottom L corner

c) – a)

TL, along good, crushed-stone track

SO, past resrs. to rd at Barley, (BW exit)

SO, across rd and TL into start.

Route 18 – Downham

Distance: 20½ miles
Off-road: 28%
Height Gain: 1550ft
Time: 3 – 4 hours
Start/Finish: Downham village, car park. GR 785 441
Maps: OS Landranger 103, Leisure Series 41
Rating: *** (when combined with Barley)
Grading: Difficult
Gradient: B

'Whistle Down the Wind'
The film, directed by Bryan Forbes and Richard Attenborough in 1961, in which local children appeared alongside Hayley Mills and Alan Bates.

Route Summary

The 'three-star' rating, when combined with Barley, says it all. Not a 'soft-touch', but every ounce of effort is surely rewarded. The bridleways are generally superbly signposted, sited and surfaced, and the settings are very fine indeed. This also provides a complete circumnavigation of Pendle – too far to comfortably manage on foot or horseback, impossible by any other means, this is a mountain bike ride par excellence!

The villages of Downham, Sabden, Newchurch and Barley enhance the wild uplands of the great hill and have been mentioned elsewhere. The area is rich in folk-lore, and there is no better way to sample it than just ambling around (assuming sufficient 'hill-legs'!), assimilating the ambience. Become a true 'countrygoer', if only for a few hours. As Richard Attenborough (as he was then) said of Downham, 'It fits the mood of the film perfectly; it is rugged countryside, grotesque, yet it has beauty – in fact it has got everything we want.'

Route Description

a) – b)

From the car park in this exquisite village, we turn right and go along the lane that leads to Worston and Pendlestone. As I rode past the quiet scene (despite being a fine Saturday afternoon in the summer) an open-top Morris 1000 came past – and I could easily have been in a scene from the film. Go past the 'Single track road' sign and Angram Farm, to a left turn into the metalled track (marked 'Little Mearley Hall'). Continue over the cattle grid

Route 18: Downham

Downham

and along the lane, a wooden bridleway sign pointing the way. A glorious track with splendid views to Pendle on the left, reminiscent of Derbyshire's Manifold Valley. Past the farm and cattle grid, continuing straight on along the semi-metalled track and over the little bridge towards the next farm. Keep ahead through the metal gate, following the line of trees, to another gate and then past the farm, bridleway arrow pointing straight on. Continue through the dog-leg and past the cottages (another sign), still on an excellent dry, stony track. If a little bumpy at times, it is flat and perfect on a mountain bike – brilliant! Through a red gate, then another, past the farm and over the little bridge to the road, 20 metres ahead at the T-junction.

b) – c)
Turn left and up the hill, following the signpost 'Sabden 2', shortly passing the 'Forest of Bowland, AONB' sign. This is the start of a long pull all the way to the saddle at the Nick of Pendle, from where George Fox is reputed to have held his sermon (see previous route). A ride all the way up here is no mean feat (not that I would know!). Past the Wellsprings Inn, so named because of its adjacent spring, a popular venue with brave souls hang-gliding or dry-skiing from Pendle's slopes.

Finally, over the saddle and the winding road begins its descent, but almost immediately we turn right into the well-marked bridleway. Through the wide gate and down the semi-metalled track. This is another fine track, although expect patches of mud – which can be avoided without too much difficulty. Go straight on, following the track past the farm and a bridleway sign. The track becomes narrower. and a little rocky, but the gradient is with us, and provides riding for the connoisseur. Through the gate, I passed plenty of grouse and pheasant. The track improves and runs more easily alongside the drystone wall. Continue straight on through the gate and farm, running out from moorland to rich lowland pasture as we slide off the tail of Pendle – I read somewhere that the hill is seven miles long! Go through a wooden gate and along the semi-metalled track, continuing the everlasting downhill past the white house, then a scattering of dwellings. Through the wide metal gate to the lane, with a storming run down to the bottom and the T-junction.

c) – d)
Turn left, following the sign to Sabden (our final, linear route goes from here to Whalley). Turn left again, and we follow the sign 'Sabden, 2' on Whalley Road. Now begins the long return, with Pendle forever on our left, passing through a quiet, agricultural valley on a fine lane, directly to the very attractive little village of Sabden. Straight on into the village, past the great horse chestnuts lining the road, by the stream and stone wall. Pass the post office and the Pendle Witch beckoning one in.

At the crossing of Pediham Road, we continue straight on up Wesley Street. Along the metalled lane around the church, making a right turn hard by it, on a track between drystone walls. Past the substantial house on the left and over a slightly muddy patch to cleaner going, to a wide wooden gate. Straight on, and along the enclosed track to the next gate. We make a right turn immediately after, running hard by the ditch and hedge. This soon leads to a footbridge across the stream, and then in 20 metres we turn left on to the fine, crushed-stone, track.

This bridleway now follows Sabden Brook along the valley, going across a couple of cattle grids, to the farm. Turn right here and go over the stream on a good track, heading up the hill on a stony and grassy path alongside the drystone wall, to a gate in 200 metres. Continue straight on, following a fine grassy track, up to a T-junction where we turn right. Up the trail between banks – a magnificent track, although the gradient doesn't allow that 'the force is with us'! This is surely an ancient 'holloway' – there are remnants of packhorse trail gritstone setts. It soon winds its way to the high wooden gate, that is the exit to the road.

d) – a)

Although the return is now entirely on-road, this is as fine as befits the route, with some testing little ascents contributing to the highly respectable height gain – especially if combined with the Barley route. Turn left and steadily uphill, going straight on with the sign ' Newchurch 2½'. Turn left at the T-junction, signed 'Newchurch 2', uphill again and straight on. Past the turn off for Roughlee – home of Alice Nuttall, who famously suffered the same fate as the 'witches' in 1612. Continue down the 17% hill to the valley bottom, following 'Newchurch, 1'. But what goes down ... and the following 17% had me gasping up Wellhead Road to the T-junction. Turn left and straight up through Newchurch and over the rise, to great views of Pendle (even in the dark!). The winding hill now makes it a rapid descent to Barley, where we continue straight on through the village, towards Downham.

There are plenty of opportunities for refreshment in Barley, including the Pendle Inn, Barley Mow and Tea Room, before the long incline which follows the sign 'Downham 4, Gisburn 7'. Finally, we go over the high point, past the bridleway of the Barley route and the 'Welcome to Ribble Valley' sign, to go straight on at the crossroads, signposted 'Rimmington 3, Twiston 1'. A terrific ride down the quiet lane leads to a T-junction where we turn left, following the sign 'Downham 2, Clitheroe'. Down the good old '1-in-6' hill, and equally steeply back up again, to reach Downham at its apogee, where its pub (Asshendon Arms), church, and manor reside, overlooking the village's thoroughfare. The view down this road to Pendle Big End is a classic. We turn left and down this road to the bottom of the village, turning right over the little bridge and back to the car park. Was it really that good, or was I dreaming?

Summary

a) – b)
TR out of Downham car park, in the direction of Worston
SO, past sign 'Single Track Rd'
TL into BW, (SP 'Little Mearley Hall')
SO, long BW, past fms, to T-jn

b) – c)
TL, (SP 'Sabden 2')
SO, long hill, past Wellsprings Inn
SO, to Nick of Pendle, begin descent briefly
TR into BW (SP)
SO, long BW, generally good surface, gently down
SO to metalled track at bottom, to T-jn
TL, (SP 'Sabden')

c) – d)
TL, (SP 'Sabden 2')
SO to Sabden, on Whalley Rd, past Pendle Witch (pub)
SO to jn
SO, up Wesley St, to parish church
TR, immed. after church, into BW
SO, thro first gate, then TR at next (by hedge and ditch)
SO, (SP BW), over footbridge to track jn
TL, along crushed-stone track, by Sabden Brook
SO, to fm
TR at fm
SO, for 200m, thro' gate to track jn
TR, follow track (holloway) up to rd

d) – a)
TL, along rd
SO, (SP 'Newchurch 2½'), to T-jn
TL, (SP 'Newchurch 2'), uphill
SO, (SP 'Newchurch 2'), downhill (17%)
SO, (SP 'Newchurch 1'), uphill (17%)!, Wellhead Rd, to T-jn
TL, thro. Newchurch, uphill
SO, over hill and down to Barley
SO, thro, Barley, past Pendle Inn, Barley Mow, Tea Room
SO, (SP 'Downham 4, Gisburn 7'), long uphill to Xrds
SO, (SP 'Rimmington 3, Twiston 1'), quiet lane to T-jn
TL, (SP 'Downham 2'), down 1-in-6; uphill
SO to top of Downham, at Asshendon Arms
TL, down thro. Downham to bridge
TR, back to start.

The Forest of Bowland

Although popular in season with locals and better-informed countrygoers, Bowland remains generally unknown, which is why it has become recognised as the Queen's 'fantasy retirement estate' – for as Duke of Lancaster she owns large tracts of land around Whitewell and Dunsop Bridge! The other major landowner is North West Water, and the countryside has a distinctly 'well-cared-for' look. This region forms the major part of an enormous upland AONB, with Pendle 'merely' an isolated offshoot.

Between Pendle and Bowland is the superb Chipping. A market-town since the 13th century, it retains an attractive face and a rich history. Although the market has long gone, it has become something of a tourist centre but in best Bowland tradition, this doesn't mean its corruption with gift shops and the like. A perfect place to begin a tour of the region, by patronising the excellent café and pubs. The glorious country lanes lead south to Longridge Fell, over which we can ride(?) on a bridleway, returning by road. Head north and we're into the heart of Bowland.

Dunsop Bridge is our centre for a route that runs up the valley into the great upland region; to the south are more hills, and the fine village of Whitewell. Dunsop has BT's 100 000th telephone box, at the centre of the British Isles! It also lies at the foot of the 'Trough of Bowland' scenic route from the west, winding alongside the shallow, boulder-strewn stream – echoing the Scottish glens. From Dunsop we travel east through Newton to Slaidburn. Undisturbed by tourism, it retains many early and interesting buildings, like the Hark to Bounty inn. This 13th-century building was called the Dog Inn until 1861. Apparently, the Rev. Henry Wigglesworth, as Master of the Hunt, was partaking of refreshment at the inn, when his favourite hound could be heard outside, eager to pursue the chase. His cry, 'Hark to Bounty!', struck the landlord, who promptly adopted it. The inn still retains the upstairs room, complete with original oak furniture, which was originally the courtroom, and is now a village meeting room. Around 1250 the Chief Court of Bowland (the 'Halmote') was held here, Saidburn having become the home of the de Laceys, lords of the manor.

Across the road is the youth hostel, the King's Arms public house until fifty years ago. With the corner shop, nearby café and public car park by the green at the bridge over the Hodder, this is a most pleasant place to pause awhile. The Old Grammar School, church and manor define this as a village of substance, but one still closely connected to the land.

The fells are within sight of the village and, once onto Croasdale Fell, nothing but wild, open moorland. One needs competence and confidence to tackle the long outings to remote spots, and an awareness of the vagaries of the weather: turning an easy jaunt into a desperate struggle with the shrug of an isobar. But the rewards, in good conditions, are uniquely those of being at one with nature and an unspoilt landscape.

Route 19 – Chipping

Distance: 15 miles
Off-road: 25%
Height Gain: 1350ft
Time: 3 – 4 hours
Start/Finish: Chipping, car park in village, near Cobbled Corner Café. GR 621 432
Maps: OS Landranger 103, Leisure Series 41
Rating: *
Grading: Difficult
Gradient: B

'Bikers' favourite – beans on toast, egg on toast, extra egg on toast, bungo soup ...'
Menu – The Cobbled Corner Café, Chipping, 1997

Route Summary

Chipping is a smashing village, one that wouldn't be out of place amongst the finest in the Cotswolds. But we have sterner business on Longridge Fell, and the couple of miles to its foot provide a gentle warm-up. The path up the hill goes surprisingly easily, for such an impressive hill from afar. An excellent track up, albeit pushing, leads through a soft descent, which requires care to preserve self, route and bike. Some great road-riding, back over the hill, leads to an 'interesting' bridleway that follows (in!) a stream, and then the muddiest stretch of these routes. The final bridleway is innocent enough, and nicely rounds off the outing. But don't start too late, or you'll miss all the other cyclists being resuscitated at the café!

Route Description

a) – b)

There is ample parking in Chipping, perhaps the most convenient being in the centre, and provided with toilets as well. Turn left and along the high street, passing (for those with extreme powers of self-control, or in the unlikely instance of it being closed) The Cobbled Corner Café. Go straight on through the village, following the sign 'Clitheroe 9¼'. The status of Chipping as a market-town since medieval times, is reflected in its pubs, as we pass the Sun Inn, Tillotson's Arms and Talbot. Another 50 metres and we are out to the glorious country that lies between Longridge Fell and Chipping – no wonder it is such a favourite with touring cyclists.

Proceed for a mile or so, then take the second right turn, which takes us

Chipping

in another mile to a T-junction. Turn right and go up the rise for a quarter of
a mile to turn left into the bridleway leading us right over Longridge Fell.
Marked with a bridleway sign and 'Rakefoot Farm, B&B', we turn steeply up
the concrete path, over the cattle grid and around the bend to the left, heading for the farm. Fifty metres from the bend and stream is an unmarked gate
into the field on the right, through which we go. Heading diagonally left-
wards, we make for the cleft in the hillside which can be discerned cutting
through the trees and over the fell. A reasonably stiff push up the long grass
of the open field leads to a wide gate. Straight on and follow the cleft, more
obvious now, running at 45 degrees up the hillside through a break in the
plantation. There are tremendous views, over the farm and the vale,
stretching away to the Forest of Bowland. Continue straight on and through
another gate in 200 metres. The obvious track narrows and becomes a little
too rocky to ride (uphill), but it's a distinguished track that leads delightfully over the top and to a fork. Turn left here, following the bridleway arrow over the top of the hill through a broad clearing in the wood.

Continue straight on, following the obvious track and bridleway signs
as we cross some forestry tracks and head down the other side of the fell,
still through coniferous woodland. Some of this descent is rather boggy,
but the gradient and a little cunning should see to a relatively easy passage,
although the track is not of the calibre of the ascent. The last part of this
track down through the wood improves, and soon the gate is reached,
marking the exit from the fell proper. Ahead lies the farm, at the bottom, by

the road. We go pleasantly down across the grass and straight on through the gate, following a faint track that becomes more evident as we approach the farm. At the low point a great mud hole exists to snare the unwary – enter at your peril! Fortunately, an easy alternative exists, and a simple circumnavigation around the track brings us to the end of a fine bridleway at the road – on the other side is the farm.

b) – c)

Turn right and along the road, keep right at the fork, following the sign 'Longridge 5'. Straight on, (past the bridleway on the left, part of the Ribchester

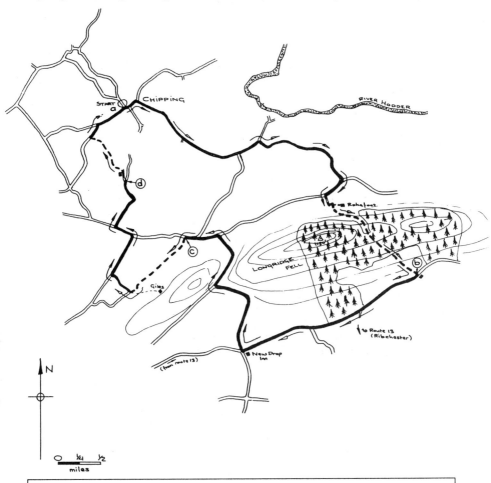

Route 19: Chipping

route), to the crossroads at the Newdrop Inn. Turn right, following the sign 'Chipping 5'. The lane undulates, then reaches the bottom of the long climb that takes us back over the tail of Longidge Fell. Once again, a brilliant northern vista from the viewing point, before the descent. At the junction we turn right, following the sign to Chipping and Whitewell. Steeply down ('20%' sign), rapidly reaching the T-junction at the bottom. Turn left, following the sign 'Chipping 3, Whitewell 5, Longridge 6'. Continue straight on, down a 1-in-8 hill, past the junction signed 'Longridge 4'. Past two footpath signs, and opposite the farm, as the road dips, we turn left into the signposted bridleway, going immediately through a shallow stream.

c) – d)

Follow the stream around. The path is regained, a little muddy, as it rises between an avenue of trees to a more grassy surface. A bridleway arrow points on as we run into an unequivocally muddy stretch, where the best option is to carry the bike for a couple of hundred metres to the good track beyond. This time there is little option other than to plod through – but as this was my worst experience of mud on any Lancashire route, then it is but small beer compared to the South! Finally, out to a good track where we turn right (ignoring Giles Farm), following the semi-metalled track easily down to the bridleway exit at the apex of the lane.

Turn right and nicely downhill to the T-junction at the telephone box. Right again, and along to the next junction. Turn left, following the sign to Chipping, and along for 100 metres. Cross the stream by the fine bridge, to turn right immediately before the Dog and Partridge, following the sign 'Chipping 1½'. Straight on, until the road curves around right as we continue straight on along the wide bridleway, signposted but not too easily seen with the undergrowth.

d) – a)

Along the semi-metalled track , making a left turn immediately after the first house (Radcliffe Cottage). The excellent gravel track leads through an avenue of trees and to another cottage, where we turn right along a grassy track that runs between bushes and beside a stream - delightful! Go up to a metal gate and into the field, keeping hard by the left hedge. Continue uphill, bearing diagonally left as we enter the larger field, to follow the left hedge again as we head onwards to its far side. The flat but bumpy grassland soon leads to the far hedge, with a gate and bridleway sign at the road.

Opposite is The Croft (bungalow) - we turn right along the lane to the T-junction, and follow the sign 'Chipping ¾'. Fifty metres further to reach the 'Chipping' sign and we're suddenly back in the village, making a left turn into the car park. Worth another sortie to the café?

Summary

a) – b)
TL out of car park, past café
SO thro' village, follow SP 'Clitheroe 9¼'
SO, out of village
2nd TR, to T-jn
TR, up rise, shortly to BW
TL into BW (SP 'Rakefoot Fm, B&B)
Follow concrete track, to L-bend, TR in 50m
Diag. L, across open field (no sign), heading for cleft in hillside
SO, cleft more clear, SO thro. break in trees
SO, over hill
TL at fork (SP, BW)
Down hill (SP, BW), soft in wood
SO, improving track, to wood exit
SO, across open fields, towards fm
SO, past mud-hole to rd (fm opp.)

b) – c)
TR along rd
Keep R at fork
SO to Xrds – Newdrop Inn
TR (SP, 'Chipping 5, Whitewell 6')
SO, up long climb and down 13% to jn
TR, (SP, 'Chipping, Whitewell'), down 20% to T-jn
TL, (SP, Chipping 3, Whitewell5, Longridge 6)
SO, down 1-in-8, SO past jn

c) – d)
TL into BW (SP)
SO, along shallow stream, fair track, to v. muddy later
SO, exiting to dry track, nr. Giles Fm, to rd
TR, on to rd, downhill to T-jn
TR, along to jn
TL (SP, 'Chipping')
SO, 100m, over bridge (before Dog & Partridge)
TR, (SP, 'Chipping 1½'), to R-bend

d) – a)
SO at bend, into BW (SP)
SO, semi-metalled track, to Radcliffe Cottage
TL, along track, to cottage, (no SPs)
TR, enclosed track
SO, then bear L, up thro. field
Keep towards L hedge, to far side field
SO, to BW exit at gate, to rd
TR along, to jn
Follow SP 'Chipping ¾'
SO to village, TL into start.

Route 20 – Slaidburn

Distance: 18 miles
Off-road: 45%
Height Gain: 2500ft
Time: 3 – 4 hours
Start/Finish: Slaidburn – car park on Clitheroe road. GR 714 524
Maps: OS Landranger 103, Leisure Series 41
Rating: **
Grading: Severe
Gradient: A

'... a strange and desolate area with a singularly beautiful heart – at Slaidburn!'
Bowland in the 19th century, as described by Edmund Vale, son of the Rector of Slaidburn.

Route Summary

The Forest of Bowland, and these routes, are worth waiting for! Good weather is almost mandatory for a successful circuit, otherwise one can encounter most unfavourable conditions in the wet, or the risk of getting lost amongst wild and remote moorland in poor visibility. But given a good spell of weather, appropriate experience and preparation, then this route will reward one with some of the best biking in Lancashire and (to misquote John Ruskin), therefore, the world!

The first crossing of Croasdale Fell is relatively straightforward, after which an escape down the valley to Dunsop Bridge is possible. Continuing over the fells to Brennand provides some entertaining riding, (and plenty of uphill pushing!) and another chance to escape down the valley. The final fell is initially less well marked, and leads to an impressive rising traverse up a steep and narrow track to the high saddle – recommended only for the experienced rider. The descent is easily followed (although not without some tricky parts), down to the Trough of Bowland road that returns through Dunsop Bridge.

The Bowland routes could be combined by continuing to Slaidburn along the Dunsop route from the Trough of Bowland, making a splendid outing for a full day.

Route Description

a) – b)

The car park is perfectly sited at the edge of this proud and sturdy Bowland village, with a green and the fast-flowing Hodder just across the road, and

Slaidburn's café adjacent. We turn right, and shortly up to the war memorial where we again turn right, following the sign 'Bentham, 12'. Over the packhorse bridge to exit Slaidburn past the manor house. We begin the climb alongside limestone walls, for this is an area with limestone knolls interspersing a gritstone landscape, although less prominent than in other upland areas. Fine riding gains height and views before a downhill past the 'Fishery', and in 50 metres a left turn into the well-marked bridleway heading for Shay House Farm.

Through the gate and along the good, unsurfaced track, straight on past the farms, over the river and on towards the fells. Pass through a wide metal gate, then another and over the stream. Keep right at the fork to go through the farm and another gate, then around the right of the farm on the track. Go through another gate, muddy in wet weather, and out to the fields. Follow the obvious track (no signs) through a gate and along the right of the field, now trackless. We aim for the far right field corner, running down to low ground with a profusion of undergrowth beyond. At the gate we go through into the unwelcoming undergrowth and through the stream bed. A short carry brings one to old, stone gateposts in 20 metres, and a more recognisable track between drystone walls, shortly arriving at a T-junction with the road.

b) – c)

Turn right and along the lane, heading uphill past the farm, to the gate across the road marking the start of Salter Fell (from which we exit on the Arnside – Slaidburn – Smithills Hall route). The sign informs that mountain rescue equipment is no longer available here – a reminder that this is remote hill country, and should be treated with due respect. Grid reference – SD 589 557, Tarnbrook. Continue straight on, and 50 metres after the gate we turn left, making an acute turn along the signposted bridleway. This is initially surfaced, but soon becomes an easily followed stony track, running up the cleft. Up to the plateau, with its gritstone boulders, the occasional marker cairn, and marker posts with remnants of yellow markings.

Proceed across the delightful (when dry!) soft, deep brown peat to the bridleway gate through the drystone wall. Through the gate, bear right, following the sign across the heather-clad moor, alive to the hooting grouse. We follow the fine, narrow track until the edge of the Whitendale Valley. The track becomes stony as it zigzags down to the valley bottom, like a miniature alpine track – making this perhaps my favourite bridleway in Lancashire. Past Keeper's Cottage to the metalled track and the farm, where we turn right for a few metres and then left, over the narrow bridge on the well-marked bridleway.

The bridleway sign points out Croasdale, Dunsop, and our route up the impressive climb towards Brennand. Follow the 'track' steeply up the hillside, a definite carry for the first 100 metres, and up to a lesser gradient on the obvious track. This section is best avoided unless dry. Straight on, following the signs to the bridleway gate in the drystone wall. Bear left after the gate, following the arrow to go across the wooden boarding that alleviates the boggy nature of this part of the route. Bear right, following the post to an improving track to open ground, across delightful (if dry!) peat moorland. As we crest the first rise, the second post has an arrow to the third marker and some potentially boggy going, although it's no problem in dry conditions. Go past a fenced off, swampy hollow – and wonder what it has consumed in ages past! Continue straight on, past another sign and to the wall, which is crossed by a ladder-stile to the left. We go through the gate on the right, scrambling down the rough terrain near the wall on our left. A few hundred metres down and we can go left, across the stream and an exit left through the a gate (muddy). Up to a good stony track, which heads for the moors. However, our route is to a track junction where we turn right, going easily downhill until Brennand Farm comes into sight. Down, through the gate, following the sign straight on, then steeply down the stony track that leads to the river crossing and Brennand. Pass through the gate and turn right through the farmyard to the gate and stile.

c) – d)

Through the next gate in 20 metres, striking straight up the steep slope for the high fell beyond, (no signs). Passing a descending party of walkers, my confidence was tested by their leader's friendly comments about an ascent by bike – 'One slip, and you're away!'. Gazing up, I could see the steep line over the saddle, and also his point. But, as usual, things are not as fearsome as they might at first appear, although obviously only intended for the experienced. Continue up the steep pastureland directly above the farm, left of a fence and up to the right corner of the next fence, bearing a little left to a wide gate. Continue straight on, steeply up (no signs), to pick up a grassy track and a few metres of pedalling! Pedal up to a bridleway gate with a footpath sign (still on the bridleway). We go a little right and then make a rising traverse left, up the narrow track that leads over the saddle.

Whilst narrow and quite steep, the track is well defined – to the extent that it is boot-width only, so a carry is necessary. With a steady shoulder the exposure should not be a problem. At the top we are greeted by flat ground and can recline amongst the splendid, soft banks of heather; a time to consume the 'emergency rations' whilst enjoying the impressive views down the valley. Straight on to the stile with a bridleway gate, and beyond follow along the right of the fence, as we begin our final descent. Follow the track down, past the marker post, then, a little more problematically, down steep ground to the path leading through a gate to open ground. Interspersed with bushes, it makes absorbing riding. Continue down to run alongside the wall on the left as another track joins and we pass another marker. Continue through the gate and past the ruined buildings. Pass a gate and along

Route 20: Slaidburn

a concrete strip to a white gate, and then another gate as we reach the sign 'Forest Operations'. Continue down the good forestry track, past the cut conifers. Through another gate, and a great swoop down to meet the road, at the end of a magnificent crossing of the fells.

d) – a)

From the bridleway, turn left, down the Trough of Bowland road to Dunsop Bridge. Pass the 'Smelt Mill', Bowland mountain rescue base, and the turning to Hareden Works (this is taken by the Dunsop Bridge route, and we could combine the routes along here for a full day's outing – highly recommended!) For the Slaidburn route, we simply continue on the road to Dunlop Bridge, going straight on to Newton. The last couple of miles are along the fine road through the valley of the River Hodder, to a last steep downhill into Slaidburn.

We pass the Old Grammar School and some fine, stone cottages to arrive at the junction in the centre of Slaidburn. Across is the unmistakable Hark to Bounty, whilst opposite is the King's House Youth Hostel. Turn right, following the sign to Settle, going straight on past the memorial and back to the start. Along with the final route, over Salters Fell from Hornby, this is surely the zenith of upland Lancashire riding.

Slaidburn (above Whitendale)

Summary

a) – b)
TR out of the car park
TR at the war memorial, (SP 'Bentham 12')
SO to the BW, 50m after the SP 'Fishery'
TL into BW, SP & Shay Ho Fm
SO, past fm, SO thro' next yard, to fields
Keep R, heading for RH far corner (no SP)
Gate in corner, wet, overgrown, go SO into water
SO, walled track improves (short) to BW exit at rd

b) – c)
TR, uphill, past fm, to gate
SO, thro. gate (Mountain Rescue info), for 50m
TL into BW (SP)
SO, along track, to top of fell, some markers
SO, following track, to steep, rocky, descent
SO, down to Whitendale, past Keeper's Cott.
SO past fm, metalled track to jn
TR and immed. TL on bridge (BW, SP 'Brennand')
SO, up steep slope (carry)
SO, boggy higher up, poss. tricky route-finding
SO, over top, alongside wall, down to gully
TL, across gully, thro. gate on track
TR at jn, steeply down to Brennand
SO over bridge to Brennand Fm yd.

c) – d)
TR thro. yard, to fell (no SP)
SO up hill, steep grass and moor, poss. tricky route-finding
SO to diag. narrow track over saddle (carry)
SO, over saddle, SPs, to descent
SO down, some SPs, steep
SO past ruined bldgs, to forestry track
SO to exit BW at rd (Trough of Bowland)

d) – a)
TL, along rd, past Smelt Mill (Mountain Rescue base)
SO, thro. Dunsop Bridge (SP 'Slaidburn')
SO, thro. Newton
SO, final steep descent to Slaidburn
TR at Hark to Bounty
SO to café and TL into car park

Route 21 – Dunsop Bridge

Distance: 14 miles
Off- road: 68%
Height Gain: 1500ft
Time: 2½ – 3½ hours
Start/Finish: Car park, Dunsop Bridge, road to Newton. GR 661 502
Maps: OS Landranger 103, Leisure Series 41
Rating: **
Grading: Severe
Gradient: A

'The Billmen of Bowland, Old Lancashire's pride,
Stood firm as their hills and the foeman defied.'
15th-century call to arms at Agincourt

Route Summary

Dunsop Bridge is at the centre of the Duchy of Lancaster's Bowland estates and a recent *Times* headline speculated that the Queen would like to reside in the area. This route is a natural companion to Slaidburn, sharing with it the way over Whin Fell, from Brennand. But the bridleway from Hareden, towards Chipping, gives it a character of its own. The first part across the lower slopes of Totridge are a little tricky to follow, but perhaps one shouldn't expect such a route to be too easy, and the ride, through the woods and down to the road, is very fine.

Slightly uncertain of my bearings and in 'glasses-misting-up-mode' on the latter fell, I met a farmer who, with not a trace of irony, greeted me in the broadest of local country accents, 'Do you think it'll rain?' In shirt sleeves, and warm conditions, I'll swear he hadn't noticed that it had been softly raining for much of the afternoon – which I suppose marks the true countryman from the visitor.

Route Description

a) – b)

From the fine car park, complete with information board and toilets, we turn right and to the village green, where a couple of shops gather by the bridge over the Dunsop. Ignoring the bridleway just before the bridge, we turn right immediately after the bridge at the sign by the memorial. Go past the houses, along The Crescent, simply following the metalled bridleway track along the flat valley, towards the hills. Pass the N.W. Water signs pro-

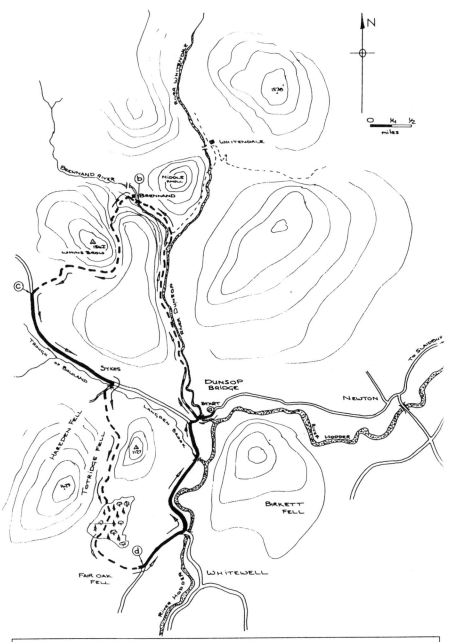

Route 21: Dunsop Bridge

hibiting vehicles, and the occasional NWW building, going over the bridge and up to the left of the river. Continue straight on, ignoring the right to Whitendale, and in half a mile go down and across the river to Brennand.

b) – c)

Turn left and up the steep, grassy hill to cross Whin Fell, as described in detail previously, (c -d, Slaidburn route). Briefly, continue straight on up the grass behind Brennand Farm to a gate which leads through soft ground and up to the rising traverse line that runs left to the saddle. A steady climb, requiring a carry. Over the top on a good track, that is well marked on its way down the other side of the fell, but not without the occasionally tricky descent. It leads down to forestry workings and the Trough of Bowland road at the bottom.

c) – d)

Turn left down the Trough of Bowland road towards Dunsop Bridge. Past the Smelt Mill, and then turn right over the bridge, following the bridleway sign, and 'N.W.Water, Hareden Works'. Follow the metalled track through mixed woodland to the stone buildings and a turn right across the bridge, running to the right of the stream. In 50 metres follow the track left over a bridge. In 10 metres, turn left off the track and on to the fell. Follow the arrow across the open, rough ground, going uphill - there is no path. Continue straight on up the hillside, opposite the farm, and bear left at the high point to go through the gate with a stile. It can be a little muddy in wet conditions. Continue up, now following a good, stony track alongside a coniferous plantation on the left. As the track fades away, the route-finding becomes a little tricky for the next mile, after which it proceeds in an exemplary manner, so don't despair! Bear a little right, going uphill, but just to the right of a cleft that runs up the hill. After gaining a little height, a wall should be found on the right. Following this uphill brings one to a track that leads to a levelling and a gate with a stile. Go straight on, following the track around to the marker post. We bear right here, following the indistinct track with the eye of faith, along a tiny ridge. It's level and we go slightly right at the stump, then diagonally across to the forest. Across the field to the drystone wall surrounding the wood, and with care we find a clough that can't be seen until one is right upon it. Down this, to find a good gate and stile crossing the wall.

Straight on through the gate and now our route-finding problems are solved, with excellent waymarking as we follow the sinuous track through the wood. Continue straight on between the wall and fence and through the gate. Follow a grassy track at the edge of the wood to another gate, and then go gently down on the faint track. Once out to open ground a metalled track is reached at the gaggle of chicken-houses, where we turn left. We follow the bridleway sign easily down the tarmac track, to turn left at the junction. Continue gently down the lane, past the cottage and rapidly to the T-junction with the road, marking the end of the bridleway. A superb run, compensating for the earlier tricky route-finding.

d) – a)

Turn left, and shortly reach the T-junction with the triangular green and bus stop. Turn left, following the sign, 'Lancaster 17, Dunsop Bridge 1¾'. Straight on past Hodder Bank, following the River Hodder towards Dunsop, and then the sign ' Dunsop Bridge,¼'. Over the bridge in Dunsop and directly back to the car park. When combined with Slaidburn, an excellent composite route for the connoisseur of remote fells.

Dunsop Bridge (Whin Fell, above Brennand Farm)

Summary

a) – b)

TR out of Dunsop car park, over bridge, to 2nd BW, at war memorial

TR into BW, past The Crescent, metalled track

SO, long, flat track up valley, past NWW bldgs.

SO, over river, fork L down to Brennand Fm

b) – c)

TL in fm yd, (following Route 20 to Trough of Bowland)

SO, uphill, steep grass and moor, poss. tricky route-finding

SO to diagonal narrow track over saddle (carry)

SO, over saddle, SPs, to descent

SO down, some SPs, steep

SO past ruined bldgs, to forestry track

SO to exit BW at rd (Trough of Bowland)

c) – d)

TL, along rd, past Smelt Mill (Mountain Rescue base)

TR, over bridge, BW SP, also 'NWW Hareden Wks'

Follow track R, then L, across stream

10m on, TL at BW SP, SO up fell above fm

(Poss. tricky route-finding till wood)

SO, up fell, bear L to track

Bear R as track fades away, keep R of clough

SO along track

Bear R, some markers

SO to wood, entering via hidden gully

SO thro. wood, good SPs

SO, downhill beyond wood to jn at chicken huts

TL, metalled track to T-jn at rd

d) – a)

TL along rd

SO to jn and bridge over Hodder

TL (SP 'Lancaster 17')

SO, following R. Hodder

Keep R, SP 'Dunsop Bridge ½'

SO, over bridge, thro. village, TL into car park

The Lune Valley

The River Lune stretches from the estuary at Glasson Dock, past Lancaster and east to Hornby (where we cross on day one of Route 27), before a long journey north, departing Lancashire around Kirkby Stephen. For me, this is one of the most scenically attractive areas (with Arnside-Silverdale AONB) of the whole glorious county. And yet it is largely overlooked – presumably because the M6 takes many fleeing-past to follow the well-trodden Lakeland paths of Wordsworth and Wainwright. This was, however, also an area well known by the Romantic poets and great landscape artists. A less well-known connection is the former village school at Cowan, where the four Brontë sisters stayed for a grim year. Now a private house, a plaque is all that remains of this past. Two of the sisters fared so badly that the resulting 'consumption' led to their tragic deaths. Charlotte and Emily happily survived, and the experience was controversially used as a model for the dreadful Lowood School in *Jane Eyre*. The heroine finds herself first a reluctant pupil, and later a teacher. Even long after Charlotte's death, the alleged slander was pursued by the head of Cowan school, showing the effect of Charlotte's writing on a contemporary society that was not always sympathetic.

Glasson Dock was formed in the 18th century, when a canal link was made to maintain the sea trade to Lancaster, as the Lune began to silt-up. Never particularly successful, the canal and its splendid aqueduct (passed on the Crook O' Lune route), were soon out-performed by the railway connecting north to south. The dock withered in Victorian times, but recently it has been re-invigorated by the leisure trade, and the canal's traffic ensures that the dock is once more an interesting and vibrant place.

Lancaster is justly Lancashire's premier city. Despite its 11th-century foundations as the seat of Roger of Poitou (awarded by William the Conqueror in 1070), the city is mostly of an attractive Georgian build. Little evidence remains of its early settlement by the Romans or Saxons as it was, for centuries, in the path of the marauding Scots, on their forays south. At least we have the castle, with some original Norman parts – although residence is now mostly dedicated to a couple of hundred 'guests' of the Crown, whose stay is not exactly from choice! However, by the millennium this function should be relinquished, and access to the castle made on a more voluntary basis. From the Tourist Information Centre, opposite the castle in the heart of the city, a number of attractions are easily reached on foot, or bike. The Lune is nearby, and links our routes – as we head south along its estuary on the return to Glasson Dock, and east along its banks to complete the Crook O' Lune route. These are a major part of an excellent cycleway project completed by the council, one that deserves wider recognition – the least we can do is make good use of it!

Route 22 – Grizedale

Distance: 8 miles
Off-road: 39%
Height Gain: 700ft
Time: 1 – 2 hours
Start/Finish: Scorton Car Park and Picnic Site, nr. M6 services. GR 505 504
Maps: OS Landranger 102, Leisure Series 41
Rating: *
Grading: Easy
Gradient: C

'The landscape today is no more natural than its walls. It was carved out by the
hunter-gatherers in late Mesolithic times, over exploited in Bronze Age times, and abandoned
by the Brigantes and Coritani.'
Richard Hodges, Wall-to-Wall History, the story of Roystone Grange, 1991

Route Summary

This is a route that contrasts dramatically with the major Bowland routes,
being short, flat (well, almost!), and a delight to follow off-road – an example for the less enlightened landowner. Be careful to note the obvious re-
striction on the way to the first bridleway, and enjoy a delightful journey up
the Grizedale Valley, on a track that is not too sensitive to conditions. It is
perhaps perfect in reverse, as a downhill ride. The bridleway beyond Fell
End Farm is well marked across pasture, leading to a pleasant return on
quiet lanes, in an area with a long history of settlement.

Although really at the edge of Bowland, it falls more naturally into the
Lune Valley character, providing a pleasant little jaunt, or a 'taster' for the
less experienced – not at all bad value!

Route Description

a) – b)

Turn left out of the excellent picnic site, albeit hardly out of earshot of the
M6. Over the motorway bridge and shortly to the T-junction, exiting from
Cleveley Bank Lane. Turn right, running near the southbound carriageway,
past Tuft Cottage (B&B). Over the M6 again and down to Scorton, going
along Wyresdale Crescent to the centre of the village. Remarkably, this picturesque and popular village lacks a traditional pub, the nearest a couple of
miles away. Go straight on past the first left in the centre, to turn left at the
next road, immediately after the bowling green. Pass under the M6 in 200

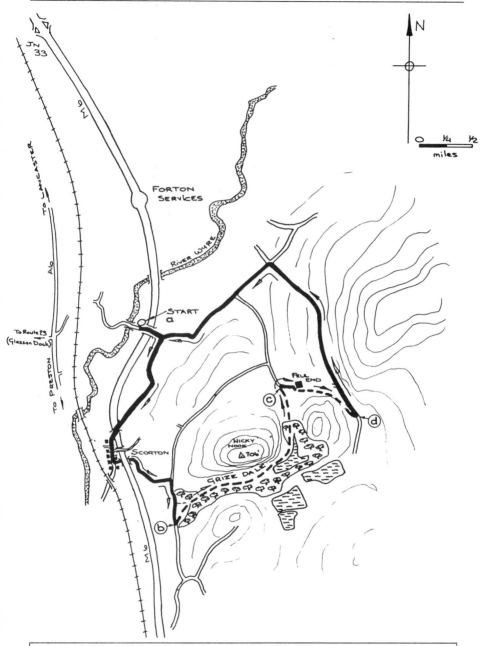

Route 22: Grizedale

Lancashire Packhorse Trail (after a display on route 10)

metres as we head up the 1-in-6 hill to the T-junction (did I say it was flat? Sorry!). Turn right and gently down. As we swing right, an appealing path presents itself at the apex – however, we **ignore** this and continue downhill to make an acute left turn at the well-signed bridleway.

b) – c)

Proceed on to the bridleway, following the sign to Grizedale Valley. The route is easy to follow and the first part is flat and grassy as it runs near the stream, then through the first gate. At the start of the woodland, the track seen earlier (footpath only) joins from the left. Straight on, through the gate and up the gentle incline, following the sign 'Nicky Nook, 1'. Along a concrete strip, straight on through the next gate and past the dry reservoir, with a profusion of rhododendron bushes that would be spectacular in full bloom. Past the path and gate to Nicky Nook, continuing along the obvious track to another gate and open ground. The track is still easy to follow as it runs along the flat, exiting through the gate to the road.

c) – d)

Turn right, and down the metalled lane directly to Fell End Farm. Continue straight on, going just to the right of the farm buildings (blue arrow on the farm wall), and past the milking parlour. Following another arrow, we go through a wide gate, and another, continuing straight on into the fields. Straight on through the gate, running to the right of the fence along an unmade track that fades away as we go gently uphill. Two hundred metres on, we turn left through the bridleway gate, following the arrow, then continue up the rise, simply following the fence on its other side. Past gateposts in 50 metres, and a bridleway sign points straight on. Across the open field to a wooden gate on the far side, a bridleway sign again indicating straight on. Our path now runs just to the right of the fence, slightly down and past a bridleway sign on a post. Pass a gate, again signed, to follow alongside the ramshackle wall and straight on through the next gate in 100 metres (no sign, for once!). The road can be seen running across 150 metres ahead. Continue, to reach the road at the small bridge, the bridleway sign proving that we have arrived at the correct spot. Top marks for the route-markers! In fact, this area seems particularly well endowed with footpath and bridleway signs – which are, after all, to the benefit of everyone, a commendable approach to countryside access.

d) – a)

Turn left and across the open moorland on the ribbon of tarmac, making for a delightful downhill run to the crossroads. Turn left to go pleasantly down to the T-junction, where we turn right and shortly reach the fork. Turn right, following the sign to Scorton Picnic Site. Back across the motorway to the start.

Summary

a) – b)
TL out of the picnic site, over the M6, along Cleveley Bank Lane to T-jn
Turn right
SO to Scorton
SO, thro. Scorton, TL immed. after bowling green
SO, under M6 in 200m, past Brook Fm
SO, 1-in-6 uphill to T-jn
TR, SO (past FP to Nicky Nook)

b) – c)
TL into BW – good SP, acute bend
SO along good BW, thro. Grizedale
SO to BW end, at rd

c) – d)
TR along short rd to Fell End Fm
SO (BW, SP), past fm on R
SO, up thro. several fields
SO, to reach moorland rd at stone bridge

d) – a)
TL along rd to crossing
TL
SO to SP 'Scorton Picnic Site'
TR into Cleveley Bank Lane
SO over M6, TR into start

Route 23 – Glasson Dock

Distance: 20 miles
Off-road: 38%
Height Gain: 400ft
Time: 2 – 4 hours
Start/Finish: Glasson Dock, marina car park. GR 445 561
Maps: OS Landranger 97, Leisure Series 41 – part only
Rating: *
Grading: Easy
Gradient: A

'There'll always be an England
Where there's a country lane,
Wherever there's a cottage small
Beside a field of grain.'
Ross Parker and Hughie Charles, There'll Always be an England, 1939

Route Summary

One of a rare breed – an 'Easy' grade! This time the gradients and height-gain really are insignificant, but the route is a fair length and provides a surprisingly satisfying run. One that I found most enjoyable on the Edwardian Triumph Roadster, bowling along with its single-speed as happily as it would have done 90 years ago. Gratifying that the changes since then have, on balance, made it a better route today – the benefit of tarmac and converted railway track outweigh the effect of traffic.

Recommended as an introductory route, but one with the challenge of a reasonably long run. One can push through the city centre without much trouble, so an early start is best to enable an exploration of this most interesting and attractive place. A visit to the Tourist Information Centre enables the castle to be seen (across the road), well worth visiting as it figures in Lancashire's history from the Norman Conquest. We return past here after the ascent of Caton Moor (on the Crook o' Lune route), to follow the Lune in the other direction. Lancaster's efforts in providing such excellent cycleways presents riding opportunities simply too good to miss!

Route Description

a) – b)

The car park is easily found, and proves a justifiably popular spot. We turn left to leave it, and immediately turn left again, over the bridge and up the

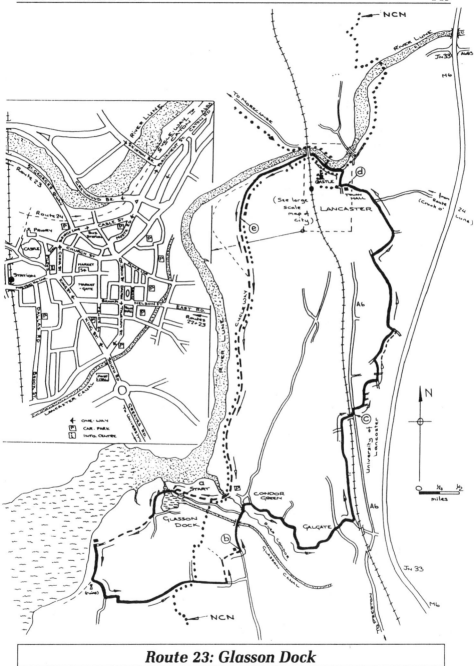

Route 23: Glasson Dock

steady slope of Tithe Barn Hill, (signposted 'Lancashire Coastal Way'). Turn left and along Bodie Hill, providing fine views over the estuary. As the road runs down and sweeps around to the left, we turn right into the signposted bridleway. The semi-metalled track heads towards the sea, straight on past Old Glasson Caravan Park. Straight on through a low gate, and another in 50 metres along a good grassy track, keeping to the right of the field. Continue straight on, following the faint track across open ground and through the gate that stands isolated in the middle of the field, at the stream crossing. Follow alongside the left hedge to a dirt track, through a couple of gates, past the farm and suddenly up to the sea. We meet the Coastal Way at the sign 'Glasson Dock, 1¾'. At the bank we can see along the coast to Morecambe and the Lakes, and inland to the Bowland hills.

Turn left and along the seashore until we meet the road, on to which we make a left turn. At this point a small stone building and rusty iron framework are all that is left of the lighthouse, or perhaps beacon. Along the quiet lane and turn left at the T-junction. Past White Cottage, now with a good view of Bowland straight ahead. Continue straight on, following the sign to Thurnham, past Bamber's Cottage, to turn left into the bridleway (sign) just before the houses.

Straight on along the semi-metalled track to the end of the field, continuing in the same line, though getting more overgrown. As the track bends left, we turn right through the unlikely gate and head through a most unpromising passage filled with metre-high grass! When we went through it looked like it had not been traversed for a long time – reason enough to persevere! Soon we reach the wide track that leads straight on along the unmetalled track, through the green gate and the enclosed way to meet the road at Aspleys Farm (care).

b) – c)

Turn left and downhill, but beware the traffic. Go over the bridge to turn right, following the sign to Galgate. This very pleasant lane winds its way straight on to Galgate. Over the packhorse bridge and the canal as it heads for Lancaster, and into Galgate. Left at the fork and to the T-junction with the old Lancaster road, leaving Leachfield Close. Turn left and head up the steady slope on the straight road, soon with views of the University of Lancaster to the right. Straight on, ignoring the 'no through road'. Past Scotchforth parish church, on the undulating road that finally runs down to meet the A6 (ugh!).

c) – d)

Turn left and along the A6 towards Lancaster (care!), taking the second right turn, thankfully escaping the main road into Collingham Park. Follow the cycleway signs along Claughton Drive, to the T-junction where we turn right. Past Barton Road Youth Centre on (surprise) Barton Road. More bike signs, (the cycle route from the university to the city) and straight on as Barton Road becomes Bowerham Road. Climb the steady incline past the Bowerham (pub), and downhill past The Park (pub). Part-way down the hill we turn right along the (one-way) Dale Street, still on the cycle route. Continue straight on as Primrose Street joins from the right, winding down past Moorlands Hotel. The Cathedral is over on the right. Continue over the canal, making a right turn immediately down Robert Street, now following the 'city centre' signs. In 100 metres, at the end of Robert Street, turn left at the T-junction along Nelson Stree. This leads directly to the Town Hall and its park across the road – not a bad place to consume one's provisions.

d) – e)

As we are now in the centre of the city, a number of alternatives exist, but I prefer to ignore getting entangled with the one-way system, and instead just walk the most direct way. We are not far from the Lune-side road that leads to the last bridleway, all the way from the city to Glasson Dock, so, on foot, we turn right immediately after the Town Hall. Walk downhill to turn left along Rosemary Lane then turn right, following the one-way system to the bus station. Turn left and then right past the W&J Pye factory, following the signs for the Maritime Museum. In 50 metres go down to the river, where we can safely re-mount.

Turn left and follow the riverside road past the George and Dragon, then Waggon and Horses, and under the railway bridge to the docks area. A sign indicates the Coastal Way. Follow the river past the Forbo factory and the Lune Industrial Estate. Straight on past the sign 'Lancashire Coastal Way', continuing along the road a little further. Eventually, past the last mill, the road simply stops, allowing riders to continue into the start of the bridleway.

e) – a)

Continue past the restrictions to prevent motors, now on the bridleway that leads back to Glasson. A straightforward half-hour's ride provides a delightful run along the perfectly flat route of the old railway. Straight on, following signs to Aldercliff. Often along an excellent cinder surface, sometimes running through an enclosed track, and in the later stages with fine views over the estuary to Glasson. Under a small bridge, past the picnic site which provides road access, as we get approach Glasson. The dedication plaque indicates that this track was opened in 1991. It certainly provides, along with its counterpart from Lancaster to the Crook o' Lune, possibly the best of the lowland off-road cycling in Lancashire.

Go straight on, over the tributary and through the gate, as we ride around the edge of the bay, with Glasson Dock a half-mile distant. After travelling south, we swing west and run alongside the wetland grass that we also find at Silverdale's shore. Through another bridleway gate and the swathe of grass alongside the road, taking us right back, past the small bowling green, to finish at the car park. A delightful outing!

Glasson Dock

Summary

a) – b)
TL out of car park
TL immed., over bridge
SO, up Tithe Barn Hill
TL onto Bodie Hill SO, along rd, at bend SO into BW (SP)
SO past Old Glasson Caravan Pk
SO thro. fields to fm
SO along Coastal Way to old lighthouse remains
TL along rd to T-jn
TL, past White Cottage
SO, SP 'Thurnham'
TL into BW (SP)
SO to unmarked gate
TR, thro. v. long grass to Aspleys Fm
SO, exit BW to main rd

b) – c)
TL along rd (care!)
SO, over canal
TR at jn, SP 'Galgate'
SO to Galgate and T-jn
TL, uphill, views of Univ. Lancaster on R
SO, past Scotchforth church, to A6

c) – d)
TR along Collingham Park
SO, along Claughton Drive
SO, cycleway SP, to T-jn
TR, along Barton Rd
SO, along Bowerham Rd, uphill past Bowerham (pub)
Downhill, past The Park (pub)
TR (cycle SP), into Dale St
SO along Primrose St, past Moorlands Hotel
TR down Robert St to T-jn
TL along Nelson St to city centre
SO to Town Hall, at lights and park

d) – e)
Follow signs, ride, or walk direct towards Maritime Museum
At River Lune, TL
SO past George and Dragon, Wagon and Horses
SO for docks rd, past Forbo factory
SO past Lune Ind Est, Keyline factory

e) – a)
SO at end rd, into BW (to Glasson)
SO, (SP Aldercliff, Coastal Way), BW
SO, past access point
SO, around bay to grass before Glasson
SO, to bowling green and TL into start.

Route 24 – Crook O' Lune

Distance: 19 miles
Off-road: 43%
Height Gain: 1800ft
Time: 3 – 4 hours
Start/Finish: Crook O' Lune, car park and picnic site, west of Lancaster and 2 miles from junction 34, M6. GR 521 648
Maps: OS Landranger 97, Leisure Series 41
Rating: **
Grading: Difficult (-)
Gradient: B

> 'On each side rise two sloping hills, clothed with thick woods, variegated rock and herbage: between them in the richest of valleys the Lune serpentines for many a mile and comes forth ample and clear ... a perfect landscape.'
> *Thomas Gray, 1769*

Route Summary

This part of the Lune Valley has long been appreciated for its superb vistas, with Turner and Ruskin, for instance, extolling its virtues. The route takes us far enough up the hill to some grand views from Caton Moor, which provides less taxing riding than might be expected. Although the climb is fairly long, it is on a good, easily-followed track, leading to an easy descent. The road-work to Lancaster is varied and provides interesting, if fairly demanding, riding. Approaching over the hill and down past Williamson Park provides a fitting entrance to the city. Finding a way through the centre shouldn't be a problem by bike. Simply make for the castle – well worth a visit when open for guided tours, between April and October. From the castle, the return (entirely on the cycleway) makes a splendid finish – well worth two stars!

Route Description

a) – b)

Amongst all of the excellent starting points from car park/picnic sites through the length of Lancashire – surely there can be none to surpass this? Not forgetting to prepare the 'inner man' at the first-class refreshment stand, we turn left, then go immediately over the bridge, and easily to the T-junction with the A683. Turn left, following the sign 'Caton ¼' past The Cottage (restaurant and tea-room) and the Ship Inn, and shortly to the small roundabout. Turn right, past Caton Methodist Church, (1836), happily off the busy road and along Brookhouse Lane. Straight on, over the bridge in the direction of the hills. Continue past the Black Bull and the fine parish church of St Paul's. Along Caton Green Road on a steady climb out of the village to the country and fine views to the left, over the Lune Valley. Downhill to rejoin the busy A683 (care). Turn right, past the 'Claughton' sign and under the bridge (over which the cable-and-bucket system from Caton passes!). Then it's on past the next aerial-ropeway to the Fenwick Arms.

b) – c)
Turn right at this crossing onto the minor road beginning the long climb to Caton Moor. At first a fine, metalled lane to the fork. Turn right on the gravel and up to a gate, then straight on up the semi-metalled track. An enclosed lane bounded by stone walls, with tarmac displaying the skid marks of horseshoes! The metalled lane continues with the possibility of riding all the way (although I found plenty of reasons not to!). Past the farm, straight on along the unsurfaced track to a T-junction.

Turn right, following the drystone wall around the edge of the wood, down a bit then up again, on a good rocky path that would be less pleasant in wet conditions. Follow the track around the wood, going left as it climbs up steeply past the bridleway sign. Up to the end of the wood, managing some pedalling, and straight on up the hillside, near the wall on a track that was in the process of 'improvement', as it leads up to the clay quarries feeding the aerial ropeways. The way is obvious (following the bucket-line!), until we reach a hairpin bend in the track – ahead the cables disappear, presumably to the loading area.

Follow the track as it bends around right and under the second ropeway, heading along the contours across the field. Shortly, however, we turn left through the first gate into the field, following the rising track up to the buildings. Pleasant riding up to the gate. Around the side of the buildings, with the wind farm windmills merrily spinning just behind. Through the second (abandoned) stone building, following the obvious track past the windmills. Over a cattle grid, to the gate in the stone wall where we take leave of the excellent bridleway.

c) – d)
To the right, the views across the Lune Valley are superb, so make sure of a fine day! On the metalled track we simply fly down to the bottom of the valley, a glorious downhill to repay the earlier height gain, but don't think that was the last uphill! At the bottom we turn left at the T-junction – there's a postbox set into the stone wall opposite. Pass the grand 'country houses' to reach the next T-junction in half a mile. Turn left, and up the steep rise. Where the road bends right, we can either follow it, or continue straight on over a walled, but unsurfaced, track. The occasional scraped stone testifies

Route 24: Crook O' Lune

to some rather adventurous efforts of cars up the rise! Down the other side, and we meet the road again at New House.

Continue straight on over the crossing, following the sign to Quernmore. Go over the bridge and up the steep, if short, hill. Over the top there's a cattle grid and a great view back to the wind farm we passed earlier. Continue past the remarkably isolated farm, through a region very similar to that between the lower Manifold and Dovedale in the Peak. Downhill steadily now, over several cattle grids and through fabulous country, with glimpses ahead of Morecambe Bay in the distance. Continue straight on to the second crossing, at the bottom of the valley, where we follow the sign to Lancaster, up the aptly named Littlefell Lane on a 1-in-5 gradient, through

Crook O' Lune (Heading towards Lancaster)

woodland to the T-junction. Turn left, following the sign 'Lancaster 1½'. In 100 metres, past the pylons, follow the road around right to see the Ashton Memorial of Lancaster's Williamson Park amongst the trees on top of the hill ahead. Magnificent riding takes us, almost without noticing, over the M6 and to the park. We pass the tall chimney and Lancaster Moor Hospital amongst the profusion of trees as we crest the rise and descend directly to the city centre. Down Queenmore Road, past Lancaster Grammar School, continuing as East Road to the traffic lights. Straight on, along Nelson Street, and we arrive at the Town Hall, as for the Glasson Dock route.

d) – e)
We follow a slightly different route to the previous one as we need to arrive at the castle, so one could simply follow the signs there. I chose to walk straight on over the lights, down the one-way street which continues as Covent Garden Street. Along to the Lancaster Market and turn right, remounting, and along King Street. Turn left at the lights, following the sign to the castle. Turn right up the rise past the Tourist Information Centre, to turn left in front of the castle, along Castle Park.

e) – a)
Follow the road around right, and Long Marsh Lane. Down to the bridge, turning right immediately before, along the excellent track. Surprisingly, there is no sign to indicate that this is the start of the upstream section of the Lune cycleway, which takes us along a magnificent track back to the start. We pass below the castle and the priory, which stand proudly at the top of the steep, grassy slope. Go straight on past the signs to the Maritime Museum, dismounting for the short bridge. Fine views over the Lune. Continue straight on along the good track, following it (dismounting) through the underpass, to go easily alongside the river. Past the road access point – which I later found an ideal parking place for an exploration of the city, (this path makes a pleasant walk to the castle and centre). Take the left fork beyond, and the excellent track continues behind the factories and under the huge stone-built Lune Aqueduct, a testament to the remarkable Victorian engineers. This bridge was built by the self-taught John Rennie! Turner painted from a parapet during its construction, for the views back to the city and its castle are impressive. I was particularly fortunate to be here in the late evening sun – which painted the bridge, river and rowing eights with gold – but able to preserve it only on film, rather than canvas. Continue straight on, under the motorway and across the road, past the old station and through a tunnel to a gate leading across the bridge over the Lune. Fork left and over the river again, making an acute right turn through a gate, and down to the gate at the road. Turn right, then immediately up and over the bridge, and back to the car park. Terrific!

Summary

a) – b)
TL out of the car park, down to T-jn in ¼ ml
TL, along A683 (care), SP 'Caton ¼'
SO to mini-roundabout; TR, follow Brookhouse Lane to Caton
SO, past Black Bull Inn to T-jn
TR, along A683, under aerial-ropeways
SO to Xrds (minor rd), at Fenwick Arms

b) – c)
TR, at Fenwick Arms, SO up steep lane
SO, to BW, to T-jn; TR, follow BW, steep in places, past wood
SO, up hillside, following ropeways
TR on track before quarry
SO under 2nd ropeway
TL thro' gate, across field to ruins
SO thro' ruins, past wind fm
SO to BW exit at gate to rd

c) – d)
SO down rd to T-jn at bottom; TL to next jn in ½ ml
TL (opp. Cransfield Cott.)
SO uphill to R-bend
SO up unmarked track, over hill (or, follow rd)
SO to jn at New Ho.; SO, along rd, SP 'Quernmore'
SO up to high point, then downhill; SO over jn
SO at jn at bottom, SP 'Lancaster'; SO up 1-in-5 to T-jn
TR, for 100m, along Littlefell Lane to T-jn
TL (SP 'Lancaster, 1½')
SO to Lancaster, over M6, past hosp.
SO, past Williamson Pk, downhill
SO Quernmore Rd, past Lancaster Grammar
SO down East Rd to Nelson St to Town Hall

d) – e)
At Town Hall square – can follow signs to castle – ride or walk
At King St, TL (SP Castle & Stn.)
TR, past Tourist Info Centre, & TL at castle
SO, along Castle Park

e) – a)
Fork R, down Long Marsh Lane
SO down track before tunnel
TR along track, past SP 'Maritime Museum, Castle, Priory'
(follow cycle-way all way back to start)
SO past access pt., then Lune Aqueduct
SO, SP 'Crook O' Lune, 3¼'
SO, under M6, past old stn.
SO, under tunnel
Fork L, over river
TR, down to rd; TR up rd, over bridge, to start.

Arnside and Silverdale

Shallow, azure waters lap around our island sands as the sun blazes down in perpetually tropical conditions, the surrounding sea teeming with shoals of shellfish, invertebrates, and plant-life. A scene familiar to the islanders of the mid-Pacific.

Recognise it now? Hardly likely, as this was the view from a much-displaced Arnside Knott, some 300 million years before man first trod here. Over millions of years, the Carboniferous Age saw the gradual deposition of this sea-life, compacting to form the carboniferous limestone that we see today, some hundreds of feet thick. Later, younger and softer rock deposits overlaid the limestone, but were weathered away, until the last Ice Age receded, some 15 000 years ago. Eventually, the vast expanse of Morecambe Bay retreated, leaving the present peninsular, its hills planed-down to their present scale. As the last ice sheets moved off, the earth's surface was severely torn, stripping the limestone bare where it had been deposited and remained as horizontal layers, places such as Hutton Roof and Farleton Crag – displaying the remarkable limestone pavements that we cross on Route 25. Occasionally, the limestone bedding plane has been thrust upright – at Trowbarrow Quarry a 100ft slab of limestone was re-set vertically, clearly revealing the imprints of fossils cast 300 million years ago. They're easily seen if one cares to climb the impressive routes!

Perhaps an atypical Lancashire landscape – for limestone underlies it all, brashly revealing itself in the huge quarry at Warton, but peeping out as friendly weather-worn crags amongst the rich undergrowth of the Warton hillside, on Crag Road. The permeability of this hard, white rock means that water can slowly dissolve it, producing fissures and caves, and homes for Stone Age man. A later claim to fame for this little village is its fine church that flies the stars-and-stripes on Independence Day, in recognition of the origins of George Washington, first president of the USA.

There's a remarkable diversity in such a tiny region, just 6 miles from east to west, and north to south. Within this, there's a heavily wooded region that provides many footpaths through extensive flora. The coastline is fringed by small crags and moss-banks, a delight upon which to wander, unless high tides prevail! Cottages and drystone walling reflect this natural landscape, with 16th-century examples in Silverdale and other villages. By contrast, Leighton Hall is an impressive country house in the grandest 19th-century English tradition – once home to the Gillow family, famous for their locally made furniture.

Leighton Moss, the RSPB reserve, is an internationally important wetland site, and attracts ornithologists from far and wide. The Visitor Centre can easily be reached from Route 26, combining a useful refreshment stop with an interesting display of local wildlife and terrain. Arnside Knott provides a particularly fine vantage point, looking over the Kent channel and towards the southern hills of the Lake District, affording some great sunsets. The sands provide an extraordinary way from Lancashire to Cumbria, traditionally Morecambe to Grange-over-Sands, but in recent times from Silverdale to Grange. An old drovers' route, it proved a worthwhile, if risky, direct way south from the lakes. The Kent channel, however, is constantly shifting – and the quicksands, combined with an incoming tide travelling faster than running speed – make a guided crossing essential.

Marking the northernmost extremity of Lancashire, this Area of Outstanding Natural Beauty provides a fitting finale to our sojourn, although we have but scratched the surface of a county as varied as the jet-black coal seams of the south and the brilliant-white limestone pavements of the north.

Route 25 – Burton-in-Kendal

Distance: 25 miles
Off-road: 40%
Height Gain: 1600ft
Time: 4 – 5hours
Start/Finish: i) Burton-in-Kendal, parking (considerately) on side roads. ii) Lay-by, opposite Four Seasons Garden Centre, on A6, 3 miles north of junction 35A, M6, (a mile due E of Burton). (i) GR 531 768, (Burton start), (ii) GR 511 763 (A6 start)
Maps: OS Landranger 97
Rating: **
Grading: Difficult (-)
Gradient: B

'On Farleton fell the pavements are open and prospects wide, from Morecambe Bay to the Lakeland hills on one hand, the Pennines on the other.'
R.B. Evans, Walking in Silverdale and Arnside, 1986

Route Summary

Although Burton is a most fascinating little town, I was unable to find a designated car park for just about the first time in Lancashire (perhaps because this is just over the border!). However, one should be able to find an unobtrusive spot by the road – worth trying as it warrants an exploration. With its quirky road names, this attractive town was once an important stop in the stagecoach days. Perhaps it is happier now to be relieved the heavy through-traffic that plies the nearby M6. Its situation below Farleton Fell makes it an excellent base for exploring this generally unrecognised region.

The alternative start is easily found, should one want to ensure trouble-free parking, as it is, after all, still in Lancashire (just!). From the M6, simply exit from junction 35, to 35A, then go north on the A6 for 3 miles. It can also be reached in a mile or so directly from Burton, across country lanes.

Although this is our longest circular route, the going is generally reasonable; potentially tricky only on parts of the first two bridleways. Off-road marking on both is negligible, until the latter part of the second bridleway – then exemplary for the remainder of the route. Apart from the initial 100 metres of the second track, the riding is on good tracks, or rough grass. And through the heart of the route across the fells to Farleton, the riding is simply superb! If time is limited, then a return direct to Burton could be made, saving a good hour. The last part, however, provides a taster for our last circular route, a little gem!

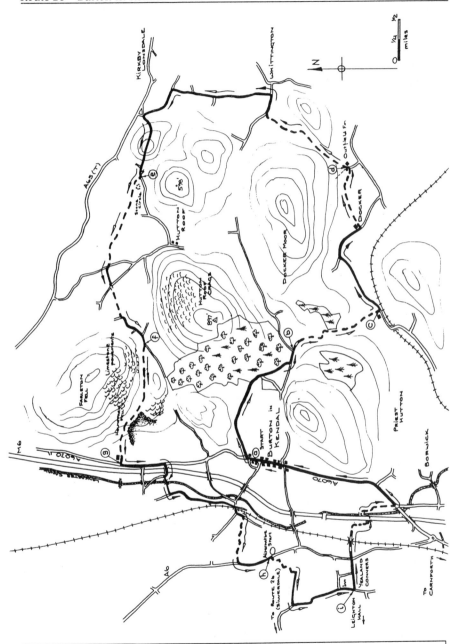

Route 25: Burton in Kendal

Route Description

a) – b)

Approaching Burton from the south, go through the village on the amusingly named Boon Walks, past the King's Arms and the Memorial Hall to the crossing of Tan Pits Lane. Turn right here, going up Vicarage Lane. Continue straight on, past Sutton Close and up the incline. Past the bridleway and along the fine lane, with improving views left over Farelton Fell towards the Lakes. After the stiff uphill, undulating riding takes us straight on through delightful woodland and finally to the T-junction. Turn left, following the sign to Hutton and Kirkby Lonsdale. Straight on, taking the second of two tracks, making a right turn into the unmarked bridleway opposite the sign 'FRPG 21'.

b) – c)

Along the broad track, and in 50 metres through a wide metal gate, following the good gravel track past the sign 'A.HAK'. Proceed on the obvious track, between drystone walls. Winding up, it continues through the gate, past the stone barn and copse, still as a good, broad track. Out to open ground, following the track past another wood and through another gate marked 'A.HAK'. Continue up the rise for 100 metres, through the gate and down the slope, then straight on through the next gate in 100 metres. Down towards the Water Board building, but turn left through the gate before the building, into the field, (no sign). Follow the faint 'holloway' (depression) diagonally downhill, heading for the left of two pylons. Go past the lone gate, left standing alone in the middle of the field, and follow the faint track-line, diagonally right and over the rise. Now along a grassy ridge, down to the fence, and through the gate marked with a footpath arrow (although a bridleway). Continue pleasantly down and across the field to pass the farm by a gate to its left. Bear right, hard by the farm, and through another gate in 50 metres, past the Alsatian, keen on tensile-testing its tether! Out to the lane, and still there's not been a single proper sign, so far!

b) – c)

Turn left, along the lane and over the stream via the stone bridge. Pass under the pylons, and at the junction turn right, following the sign to Newton and Arkholme. Straight on, and past the 'Docker' sign in 100 metres. Continue down the '15%' slope and past the farm and cottages. Turn hard left by the next farm, at the end of the stone wall and opposite the last cottage on the right before the end of the hamlet. Again the absence of a sign makes for hard work locating the proper track. This one begins through the wide gate adjacent to the building, then immediately through a very muddy stretch that warrants a carry to the next gate, going alongside the stream for 50 metres. Go straight on, and in another 50 metres the situation improves as we reach decent grass, following the fence on the right. Keep ahead through a wide gate, gently uphill, to the right of the field on a grassy track. Although short, the bumpy grass makes for hard work. It's not too far to better things, but first we continue straight on over the rise and make for the far right corner of this field, with the farm beyond. In the corner we find (fancy that!) a bridleway gate, albeit unmarked. Turn right through the gate and directly to the farm building in 150 metres. Keep hard by the building and through another gate in 100 metres, going around the building to a good gate leading into the immaculate yard of Oldfield Farm.

c) – d)
Go straight on across the hard-surfaced yard, past the monkey-puzzle tree, to take the right of two paths, a fine, concreted track with a bridleway sign – at last! Continue straight on along the excellent track and through a gate in 200 metres, then another after a further 200 metres. Continue down, through another gate and past the bridleway sign marking its end – making up for the previous difficulties. Continue along the semi-metalled lane and past the gate to Whittington Hall – I amused myself racing the pheasants. Next it's over the narrow bridge and to the junction, going straight on (signed to Kirkby Lonsdale). Straight on, past the hall's gatehouse, adorned with friendly 'keep out!' and 'electrified fence!' signs. Then downhill, to turn left immediately before the church. Up the tiny, high-banked lane, marked 'unsuitable for heavy goods vehicles' – a statement of the obvious?

Steeply up – this is surely the essence of riding in country lanes – past the renovated Lane House Farm, and to the T-junction. The signpost points to Kirkby Lonsdale, Hutton Roof, Barton and Whittington, and we turn right to follow Kirkby. Bear left at the fork, (from the road down to Kirkby), and gently up the lane, over the rise and down to the T-junction. Turn left and on to another T-junction, meeting the 'Cumbria Cycleway' signs. Left, following the Hutton Roof sign, up the longish hill, then down the other side. Continue past the lane on the right and the footpath to High Biggin, then turn right at the (partly obscured) sign 'bridleway to Hollin Hall and Sealford'.

d) – e)
Straight on through two gates, heading out to the open field. Shortly we bear left, abandoning the track that continues towards the hilltop wood. We follow the faint track across good, grassy riding, and then in the same line through a gate in 200 metres. Amongst the odd limestone outcrops, we come to the ancient 'settlement' ring, marked on the OS map. About 30 metres in diameter, its low standing-stones mark it out as an encampment. The track continues through the gate in the drystone wall, following the same line. Past the marker post (a big hole for the unwary!), and along the line of the marker posts to a wooden gate. Beyond, we follow the obvious walled track down super riding to a semi-metalled lane, just wide enough for a vehicle.

Over the bridge and to the hamlet, continuing steeply up the small, sunken lane. Proceed to a crossing where we go straight on, following the sign to Newbiggin and Farleton, where the Cumbria Cycleway departs.

Ahead, Farleton Fell can be seen at last. The metalled lane is followed until it swings right, where we continue straight on – at a junction of several walled tracks (no signs). Keep ahead through a couple of gates and into the field, heading directly for the farm across the dip. Through a gate in 200 metres to a good farm track, and the gate at the barn. Continue past the farmhouse and the bungalow, and up the steep metalled lane to the crossing at the top, going straight on, (signed for Burton and Carnforth).

e) – f)

Continue for 100 metres, then turn right, following the bridleway sign 'Limestone Link, Holme Park'. Pass through the gate, following the line of the arrow diagonally across the fell. A vague track leads just right of the telegraph pole to a good track (marker post). This is a high point, and on the right we can see part of the extensive limestone 'pavement', a rare example of this geological formation which only occurs beyond here in the Yorkshire Dales and The Burren, Northern Ireland. Over the rise and gently down through the gate, straight on then bearing right. Through the gate and around the lip of the huge quarry on the left (hidden by the line of trees). Running down, off the plateau, is excellent riding – go through a gate, and down a little 'canyon' then through the metal gate, (bridleway sign). A cracking descent is completed down a walled track and through the gate at the farm. Another gate takes us directly to the road. Excellent!

f) – g)

Turn left along the A6070, which would take one directly back to the start if time is short – if not, follow me! Turn right at the sign 'Milnthorpe, Holme ¾', (B6384). Past the Smithy Inn, over the M6 and just beyond the 'Holme' sign, turn left down Sheernest Lane. Continue over a bridge and easily down to the T-junction. Turn left, along Station Road, and past the inviting Dutton Arms. Go straight on, and then turn right at the T-junction, following the sign to Hale and Beetham. Under the railway bridge , keep left at the fork. Arnside Knott is now visible in the distance. Pass under the pylons and then turn right into a walled bridleway immediately before the farm – no sign. Fork right and go along the magnificent, enclosed, narrow track, riding all the way, to suddenly emerge on to the A6 (care!).

Turn left and along the A6 to the Four Seasons Garden Centre. Just beyond, on the right, is a lay-by – the alternative start.

g) – h)

Turn right immediately before the lay-by into the narrow bridleway, signposted 'Nineteen Acre Lane'. Another delightful track provides compelling riding to the next road. Turn right and along the road for 100 metres, then left into the bridleway marked 'Yealand Redmayne' – for now we are in the Arnside and Silverdale AONB, and the path marking is of a very high standard indeed. Another fine track (is there any other sort in this area!), goes right before the metal gate, then left at the next gate and out to the lane.

Right along Well Lane to the main road, where we turn left along Footeran Lane.

h) – a)
Up the hill to Yealand Conyers and turn left, opposite the sign 'Leighton Moss Nature Reserve, 2¾, Leighton Hall, ½'. Continue down the lane as it leads across the railway. On the far side is a bridleway sign at the start of the semi-metalled track leading up the hill. Continue straight on, running alongside the drystone wall towards the motorway and going through the gate at the top left corner of the field. We now go right, along the bank parallel to the M6. Follow the fence, and then drop down to the gate which leads underneath the motorway, and up the cutting on the other side. Through the gate and over the small bridge, then turn right along the hedged track, through the gate to the track T-junction. Turn right and down through the muddy farmyard, a series of gates, and out to the road. Across is Longland's Hotel.

Turn left, heading back to Burton on the A6070, straight on past the first right, (which is the way for the epic, final Arnside – Slaidburn – Smithills Hall route). We simply follow the road (no problem if not too busy) the mile or two into Burton, then straight through, past the King's Arms, as described at the start. Not tired yet?

Burton-in-Kendal (starting the first bridleway)

Summary

a) – b)
From Boon Walks, going N on the A6070 thro' Burton,
TR up Vicarage Lane, long hill
SO to T-jn (fair way)
TL, SP 'Hutton Roof & Kirkby Lonsdale'
TR into BW track (no SP), opp 'FRPG 21'
SO, past sign 'A.HAK'
SO, long track, finally over hill toward bldg.
TL thro' gate part-way down, follow dip L
SO in line of grassy mound/dip, to fm, (no SPs)
SO to fm and rd, BW exit

b) – c)
TL along rd, to T-jn
TR (SP 'Newton, Arkholme') for 100m
SO, past 'Docker' sign, past fm
SO, past cotts. & fm
TL into BW (no SP), muddy yard, by stream
SO, track improves soon
SO across unmarked open fields to far RH corner
TR, thro' BW gate(!)
SO, alongside bldgs. & another gate in 150m
TL into yard of Oldfield Fm

c) – d)
SO across yard, past monkey-puzzle tree
SO into BW (SPs – now OK), concrete track
SO, track & SP, leads onto lane
SO to T-jn, SO (SP 'Kirkby Lonsdale')
SO, past Whittington Hall
SO, downhill, almost to church
TL, steeply up narrow lane, 'Unsuitable Heavy Goods'
SO, past Lane Ho. Fm. to jn
TR, (Kirkby Stephen) to fork
Bear L to T-jn
TL to T-jn (Cumbria Cycleway)
TL, (SP 'Hutton Roof')
SO, up & down steep hill

d) – e)
TR into BW (SP 'Hollin Hall & Sealford')
Bear L across fields, past 'settlement' (stone circle)
SO, past marker posts, down to walled track
SO, leading down to narrow lane & hamlet
SO, steeply up to Xrds
SO (follow SP 'Newbiggin & Farleton')
SO at jn of walled tracks (no SP)
SO alongside wall to fm, and rd
SO up steep rd to top, Xrds
SO (SP 'Burton, Carnforth'), for 100m

e) – f)

TR into BW (SP 'Limestone Link, Holme Pk')

SO along track, several jns, past quarry

SO, over high plateau and down 'canyon'

SO down, thro' farmyard to rd

f) – g)

TL, along A6070

TR, SP 'Milnthorpe', B6384

SO, over M6 to jn

TL, down Sheernest Lane, to T-jn

TL, along Station Rd, past Dutton Arms, to T-jn

TR, to next T-jn

TR (SP 'Hale, Beetham)

Keep L at fork

SO, under pylons, to unmarked BW, before fm

TR along walled BW, narrow, to rd (A6)

TL, along A6 (care!) to Four Seasons Garden Centre

g) – h)

(alt. start in lay-by)

TR into BW (SP 'Nineteen Acre Lane')

SO to rd

TR along rd for 100m

TL into BW, SP 'Yealand Redmayne'

SO, hedged track to lane

TR along Well Lane to main rd (Footeran Lane)

TL, along Footeran Lane to Yealand Conyers

h) – a)

TL (opp. SP 'Leighton Moss 2¾, Leighton Hall ½')

SO, over railway, into BW

SO, around & under M6 on BW, up & over bridge to T-jn

TR, down to fm

SO, thro' muddy fm yd to rd

TL (opp.'Longlands Hotel'), along rd

SO, along A6070, to Burton

SO, into Burton, past King's Arms; Royal Hotel, on Boon Walks, to start.

Route 26 – Silverdale

Distance: 17 miles
Off-road: 26%
Height Gain: 1100ft
Time: 3 – 4 hours
Start/Finish: Car park, Arnside Knott, (1 mile south of Arnside). GR 450 774
Maps: OS Landranger 97
Rating: **
Grading: Moderate
Gradient: B

> 'Such wide plains of golden sands with purple hill shadows, ... wandering filmy clouds ... the
> great dome of the sky ... one is never disappointed in coming back to Silverdale.'
> Elizabeth Gaskell, 1858

Route Summary

We rode this route on brilliant, late autumn days, enjoying a short holiday based at Arnside Youth Hostel – equipped with everything for the riders' needs – such as bike shed, drying rooms and plenty of food! Arnside is a little seaside town with a quiet charm, and noted for stunning sunsets over the Kent estuary. An excellent centre for exploring this remarkable AONB, which includes the fine coastline around Silverdale and a remarkable profusion of footpaths that would repay many visits. Well-known as a 'twitchers' paradise, the visitor centre and RSPB reserve at Leighton Moss shouldn't be missed – it's noted for its bitterns, but it takes an expert eye, patience and a lot of luck to spot one standing almost invisibly in the tall reed-beds.

The wooded and hilly terrain gives one the impression of a much more extensive area than might appear from the ma. A remarkable range of flora is especially dramatic in spring. The riding is simply superb – easy route-finding, fine country lanes and fabulous tracks, with plenty of opportunity for refreshment stops. Pick a fine day, a low tide, and a bike is perfect for exploring the bridleways and lanes in this little gem of an area!

Route Description

a) – b)

Turn right from the car park sited below Arnside Knott. With views over the Kent estuary towards the southern Lake District, this rivals the previous route for the finest starting point. Better still, stay at the superb Arnside

Youth Hostel and enjoy a delightful three-quarter mile ride to this point. Follow the excellent track in the National Trust woodland, going through the gate and then gently down to another in 100 metres. Continue up then down, and through gates – with little difficulty, following the bridleway sign for Arnside Tower. Exit the wood at the road.

Turn right at the road, following the sign 'Silverdale'. A downhill leads to a left bend before Silverdale. Turn right at the apex, down a broad track that soon reaches a gate, leading on to the cove and shore. Continue down to the shore – in a rather fine situation. In case of a high tide, this section can be avoided by continuing through the village on the previous road – but this shore ride is too good to miss under normal conditions! With the limestone cliffs and caves to the right, we follow the general track line left, by the small cliffs, in a glorious half-mile of winding around a maze of runnels. Follow the ramp that leads left, up past the signpost, to the village of Silverdale.

b) – c)

Over the cattle grid and follow Shore Road up past The Silverdale Hotel to the T-junction. Turn right, following the sign 'Gibraltar $\frac{1}{4}$, Carnforth $4\frac{3}{4}$'. We're now on the Lancashire Cycleway. Along Lindeth Road, with a left turn before Gibraltar Farm, along Hollins Lane (following the sign to Carnforth). Continue past the Wolf House Gallery, reputed to be the place where the last wolf in England met its match (and why not!). If open, call in, it's a good café! Continue to the T-junction and turn right. Right again at the next junction – with the grass triangle – following the sign 'Carnforth $3\frac{1}{4}$, Warton 3'. Go straight on, over the railway and the river bridges, to Crag Foot. Keep left at the fork at Moss House Farm, by the square smelt-chimney. Continue up Crag Road, through the wood on a steady climb.

c) – d)

The long climb takes us to the crest of the road, although views seaward are limited by the woodland, to turn left into the well-marked, broad track. Follow the white, stony (limestone country) track up the steady incline, deep into the woods. A fine, rideable track (for the energetic!), going straight on over the top, between drystone walls. Continue downhill, gradually steepening to an absorbing final descent to Potts Cottage at the bridleway exit to the road. A truly magnificent ride! For the less experienced, a push will see one safely down the last part.

d) – e)

Turn left and go along a few miles of fine lanes to the next bridleway – but there are a few hills! Uphill to pass the private entrance to Leighton Hall, then down the 1-in-5 to the T-junction. Turn left, towards Yealand Conyers, going downhill. Past the New Inn at Yealand Conyers, and straight on following the sign 'Arnside $4\frac{3}{4}$'. Into Yealand Redmayne, now along Foot-

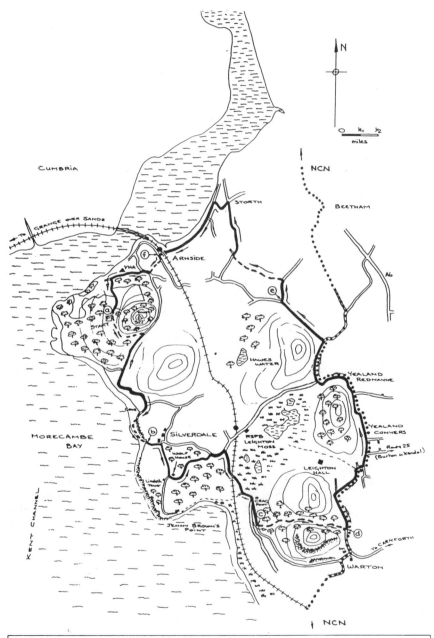

Route 26: Silverdale

eran Lane, and follow the main road which becomes Silverdale Road. Through the delightful village of Redmire, with its old limestone-walled cottages, continue along Silverdale Road to the junction. Turn right, following 'Beetham 3, Arnside 3½'. Turn left at the next junction, signed 'Arnside 3'.

e) – f)

Go pleasantly down to turn right off the Arnside road, at the sign 'Beetham 1½' (straight on is 'Silverdale 2, Arnside 2¼'). Proceed over the little bridge – a most picturesque scene with the broad oak and cottages nearby. Continue up the hill to the wood. At the top of the first rise we turn left into the excellent woodland bridleway, following the prominent sign 'Public By-Way, Dollywood Lane'. The walled track leads easily down, all the way! The glorious ride terminates at the road, with a similar sign.

Turn right, along the road for 100 metres, going straight on over the crossing and up the steep rise through the enclosed road, where I passed literally dozens of pheasants ambling around. Down to the crossing in Storth, where we turn left, following the sign to Arnside. Then steeply down the winding road to the T-junction. Turn right along Carr Bank Road, and in 250 metres follow around to the T-junction with Sandside Road.

Turn left, following the sign to Arnside. Two hundred metres along this flat, fast road there is a good lay-by that would make a perfectly good alter-

Silverdale (the Cove)

native starting point. We continue along the B5282, shortly going under the railway bridge, and immediately out to the T-junction.

f) -a)

Turn left along for 50 metres, and turn right into the track next to the bungalow. Well signed as 'Bridleway to Silverdale Road', although a little obscured. Through the gate and steeply up the fabulous enclosed track, just about rideable, but worth a push in parts. Over the rise and along the flat to emerge in the lane, going past the terrace to the T-junction in 50 metres. Turn right along Silverdale Road, following the Cumbria Cycleway, and then turn left along Redhills Road, following the sign to Arnside Knott. Go straight on, passing the excellent youth hostel in half a mile. Further on turn left, following 'The Knott' sign. Steeply up the lane, through the gate marking the beginning of National Trust land. Continue on the metalled track, over the cattle grid and gate, and along the unsurfaced track to the car park. A fitting finish to the circular routes' itinerary!

Summary

a) – b)
TR out of car park, SO thro' woods on BW to rd
TR, SP 'Silverdale'
SO, towards Silverdale, t; L-bend apex
SO, into track to cove
TL, following cliffs along seashore
SO, ½ml to exit at Silverdale village

b) – c)
SO, past Silverdale Hotel to T-jn (Shore Rd)
TR along Lindeth Rd, (SP 'Gibraltar ¼')
TL, along Hollins Lane, SP 'Carnforth'
SO, past Wolf Ho. Gallery, to T-jn
TR, along to grass triangle
TR, SP 'Carnforth 3¼', to Crag Foot
TL at fork, up Crag Rd (SP 'Warton 2')

c) – d)
SO to top of hill, at BW to woods; TL into BW (SP), good track
SO, over rise, steeply down to rd, (Potts Cott.)

d) – e)
TL along rd, past Leighton Hall
SO, down 1-in-5 to Yealand Manor, & T-jn
TL, to Yealand Conyers
SO, past 'New Inn', SP ('Silverdale, Arnside 4¾')
SO, along Footeran Lane, then Silverdale Rd to jn
TR, SP 'Beetham 3, Arnside 3½'; SO, to jn
TL, SP 'Arnside 3'
SO, to jn

e) – f)
TR, SP 'Beetham 1½', over stream, uphill
SO to top of hill, at wood, and BW entry
TL into BW (SP 'Public By-Way – Dollywood Lane')
SO, down excellent track to exit at rd
TR, along rd, SO at 1st crossing, to next Xrds
TL, SP 'Arnside', steeply down to T-jn
TR, along Carr Bank Rd for 250m to T-jn
TL, along Sandside Rd (B5282), SP 'Arnside' (alt. start in lay-by)
SO, flat rd, past lay-by, and under bridge to T-jn

f) – a)
TL along rd for 50m to BW entry
TR into BW (SP 'BW to Silverdale Rd')
SO, up enclosed track, over top to lane
SO to T-jn in 50m
TR, along Silverdale Rd to jn; TL along Redhills Rd
SO, past YHA, (SP 'The Knott')
SO, into National Trust land, on BW
SO, uphill to car park, start.

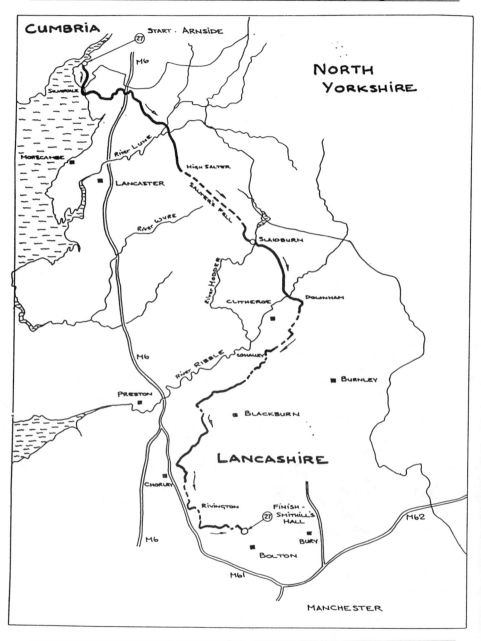

Route 27

Route 27 – Arnside to Smithills Hall

	Day 1	Day 2	Total
Distance	35ml	51ml	86ml
Off-road	36%	27%	26ml
Height gain	3020ft.	4150ft.	7170ft.
Time	6 – 9hrs	8 – 10hrs	
Start	Arnside, YHA	Slaidburn, YHA	
	Redhills Rd.	GR 711 525	
	GR:452 784		
Finish	Slaidburn	Smithills Hall, Bolton.	
		GR 698 118	
Maps	LR 97, 103.	LR 103, 109	
	LS 41	LS 41, Explorer 19	
Rating	***		
Grading	Severe (long)		
Gradient	B		

'When I stand at the beginning of one-hundred miles of moor, mountain, valley and meadow, I am standing on the threshold of a dream.'
Mike Cudahay, Ultra-distance fell runner, Mountaineering Conference, Buxton, 1991

Route Summary – Day 1

A day of tremendous contrasts – with some of the finest riding in Lancashire, literally from the seashore to the ancient trail across the wildest part of the Forest of Bowland, reaching a height of 1353ft across Burn Fell. The route starts quietly, through the wooded slopes of Arnside Knott, to a brief foray along the shore at Silverdale Cove. The village makes a pleasant stop for early re-fuelling, then a foretaste of the hills as we cross the woods at Warton Crag on a brilliant track. Delightful roadwork to Yealand Conyers, a short bridleway to take us safely under the M6, and a longer stretch of roadwork, leaves the first AONB far behind as we reach the Lune Valley.

Across the last Lune tributary at Hornby, this also marks the last opportunity for refreshments before Slaidburn, as we begin the climb to the high pass in half a mile, at Butt Yeats. The metalled lane continues as far as High Salter Farm, which gains us most of the height. What remains is a steady rise to the high plateau, following one of the finest moorland crossings in England. The route is easily followed, and generally an excellent surface, but don't underestimate its remoteness. Given appropriate preparation and fair conditions, it provides a fitting climax to the day!

We soon descend to the roads and an easy run remains, mostly downhill, to the welcoming sight of Slaidburn – like an oasis in the desert! Here there is the café, stores, Hark to Bounty, and youth hostel. Relax – tomorrow is a long day!

Route Description – Day 1

a) – b) (as Route 26)

From the youth hostel on Redhills Road, Arnside, the route follows 'Silverdale' (Route 26) to Yealand Conyers, and a more detailed description can be found there. Basically, we follow the road signed to Arnside Knott through the wood on the bridleway, and turn right for Silverdale along the road. Just before the village, turn right down the track to the cove, then left below the cliffs for half a mile, to turn left into Silverdale – in case of a high tide, the road can be followed instead. Go past the Silverdale Hotel and turn right along Lindeth Road, left along Hollins Lane, right at a T-junction, then right (signed 'Carnforth 3¼'). Straight on to Crag Foot, by the square smelt chimney. Turn left, up the steep road to the high point, and turn left up the

Stage 1, Day 1 (Silverdale Coast)

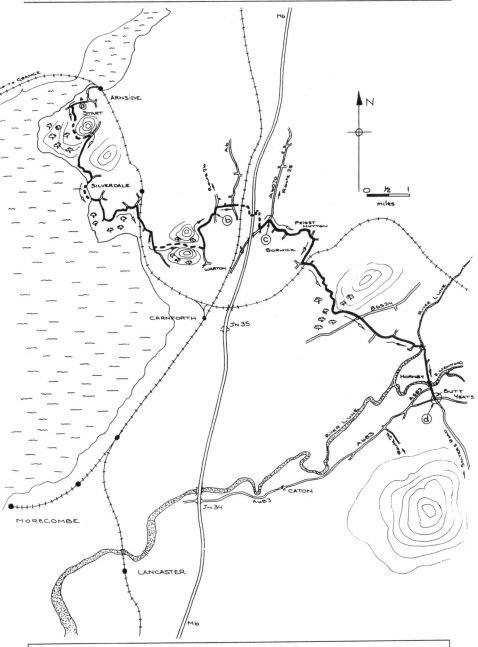

Route 27: Day 1, Stage 1

Route 27: Day 1, Stage 2

bridleway (signpost). Through the wood on the bridleway, then steeply down to the road. Turn left and follow the road past Leighton Hall to the T-junction, and left to Yealand Conyers.

b) – c) (as Route 25)

Take the first right turn in 200 metres, then straight on over the railway and up the bridleway to the cutting at the M6. Go right, then under the motorway, up the other side and turn right. Right again, and down through the farm to the road – opposite Longland's Hotel. Turn left, along the A6070, to the first right turn (signed 'Priest Hutton').

c) – d)

Go straight on to Priest Hutton. At the green (triangle of grass), turn right, follow signpost 'Borwick'. Continue straight on to the next junction, turn left uphill, then proceed, undulating, to the T-junction. Turn left, over the railway and straight on, past the sign to 'Capernwray Hall', then the house itself. Follow a long, uphill, winding road, then a very pleasant lane past forestry land. Downhill to a T-junction. Turn left, following the sign 'Kirkby Lonsdale 7'. In 100 metres, turn right (signed 'Gressingham 1, Hornby 2½'). Straight on to Gressingham, through the village and over Loyn Bridge (River Lune) to a T-junction. Turn right along the A683, and through Hornby, past the Royal Oak. Go straight on (the main road goes left), following the sign 'Wray 1½' along Station Road to the crossroads of the B6480. This is Butt Yeats, ahead is signed 'Roeburndale West'.

d) – e)

Straight on from Butt Yeats, starting a long climb, then follow a steep dip and a long ascent past Lower, Middle and finally Higher Salter Farm. Here, the tarmac lane ends and the tremendous high-moorland track crosses the fells to Slaidburn. A long, but given reasonable conditions and time, enjoyable ride over one of the finest upland tracks in England. Fortunately, the route is straightforward, simply following the track south-east as it makes a steady ascent and continues as an excellent track across the high plateau. After passing the footpath to Croasdale, there is half a mile of intermittent mud-holes, created by idiots with motors. With a little cunning these can be outflanked on the moor. We escape to the good track beyond the gate, that leads straight on down past the bridleway to Whitendale, near the beginning of the Slaidburn route. Just beyond, we continue through the moor gate, and down the road towards Slaidburn – nearly there! Down to the T-junction. Turn left and on for the last mile into Slaidburn, the last part steeply down to the junction with the Hark to Bounty on the left. Ahead is the King's House Youth Hostel. Quite a ride, and another one to look forward to tomorrow!

Route Summary – Day 2

Whist the off-road is certainly less taxing than on the first day, the roads more than make up for it – perhaps it's a good thing there isn't a third day! The initial run to Downham is hilly, as befits its leaving of the main Forest of Bowland AONB, but the country is fine and villages welcoming. Downham provides a convenient stop before tackling the major hill of the day – to the Nick of Pendle.

The bridleways between Downham and Whalley are very fine, presenting no particular problems (part of the Downham route). After Whalley (a tempting stop!), the climb to the Nab presents the steepest and most awkward section for a tired body, but is short and soon leads to superb tracks around the reservoirs. The road miles are relieved by a fine bridleway near Billinge Hill, before the grind from the outskirts of Burnley along the A674. Eventually, an escape back to country lanes can be made shortly before Chorley.

We are now on the last lap, as we pass the immaculate hamlet of White Coppice and arrive at the West Pennine Moors. The Rivington route is finally reached, its bridleway leading us up past Healey Nab and then down superb tracks to Anglezarke Reservoir. Following the first-class paths at Rivington, we make a short diversion to the return leg of the first route (Barrow Bridge). A stiff climb up from Horwich is needed to gain the flanks of Winter Hill, leaving a little more road-work to the last easy bridleway, which brings us almost to the finish. Not a bad effort for a weekend!

Bolton railway station is a couple of miles further on.

Route Description – Day 2

e) – f)

From the youth hostel, turn right and follow the 'Settle' sign on the Hark to Bounty, along the B6478. Keep right at the memorial junction, past the café and car park, to cross the Hodder as we depart Slaidburn. The hill-climbing begins straight away, with a 13% ascent which includes a hairpin bend. Go straight on for a mile, then fork right off the main road, following the Grindleton sign. Continue uphill to the T-junction and turn left, following 'Grindleton 6'. Continue up a long hill to a high point with tremendous views. Down to the T-junction in Grindleton. Turn left, following 'Chatburn 1¼', at the Buck Inn and Duke of York. Down the 1-in-7 to turn left at bottom, signed 'Chatburn 1'. Proceed over the Ribble and through Chatburn on Bridge Road to the T-junction. Turn left, following 'Gisburn 5¼', and then turn right in 100 metres, having passed the Black Bull Inn and Brown Cow. Go up the rise following 'Downham 1', and a faded Lancashire cycleway sign. A deceptively arduous uphill takes us past the imposing Methodist church, and far above the busy A59.

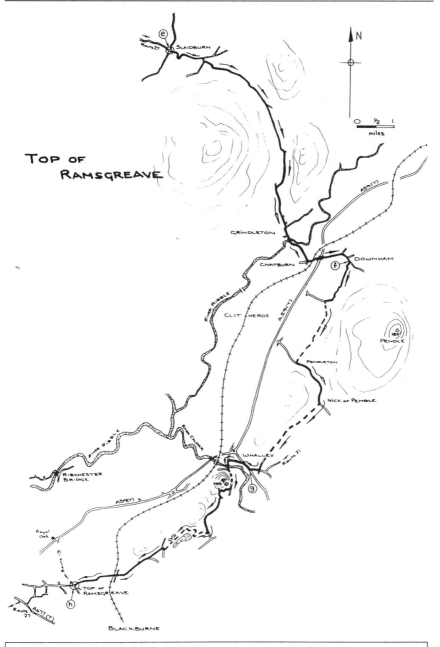

Route 27: Day 2, Stage 3

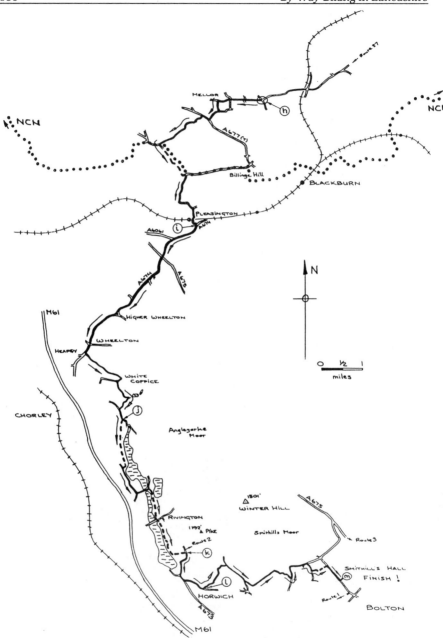

Route 27: Day 2, Stage 4

f) – g) (as Route 18, a) – c))

Over the rise to Downham, and past the Assheton Arm. Bsear right to run through the village, with Pendle framing the view. Turn right over the bridge (and past the car park of the Downham route), towards Worston, and the 'single track road sign'. Turn left into the bridleway track, signposted 'Little Mearley Hall'. Continue along the excellent track running parallel with Pendle's axis for a couple of miles to Pendleton, emerging from the bridleway to a T-junction.

Turn left (signpost 'Sabden 2') and up the long hill that leads past the Wellsprings Inn to the saddle point at the Nick of Pendle. Tremendous views! Just over the top, turn right into the well-marked bridleway. Semi-metalled at first, it becomes more basic but the gradient is favourable and leads us along for a couple of miles to the continuation lane. Continue all the way to the T-junction. At this point we depart the Downham route, but pick up Whalley (Route 14), in half a mile.

Go straight on, ignoring the left to Sabden, then turn right and along the B6246 to the T-junction with the A671.Turn right along the dual carriageway for 100 metres, to the lights. Tturn left, on the descent that starts the Whalley route.

g) – h) (as Route 14, a) to d))

Downhill into Whalley, to the mini-roundabout. Turn left at the Dog Inn, along King Street and over the Calder. Turn left up Moor Lane for 100 metres, then left up the steep, narrow bridleway. Follow the bridleway through a wood over the Nab to join the lane. Go past Whalley Banks Farm, along Dean Lane. Straight on (hilly) to a T-junction and left turn. Continue for 200 metres to a junction where we turn left, continuing straight on along Shawcliffe Lane. Turn right into a bridleway. This is a good track, but there are no signs (however, it's 200 metres before the T-junction).

Follow the very good track towards reservoirs then turn right to go down and across their head. Turn right at the bottom, following a short bridleway detour to the far side of the reservoir to meet the main track. Turn right along the main track, uphill for 100 metres then turn left, following a bridleway sign alongside the reservoir. Past the wood, keeping basically straight on, then trending a little left to exit the bridleway at the gate. Turn right and uphill to an acute left turn. This runs down York Road to bear right on to the main road, then through suburbia on Parsonage Road. Straight on across the A666 at the Rising Sun (lights), and begin the long hill that finishes at the Top-of-Ramsgreave. We continue straight on, past the Spread Eagle, along Higher Ramsgreave Road (where the Whalley route departs for the Ribble).

h) – i)

Go straight on, downhill through the village of Mellor, past the Trader's Arms, and then turn left at The Millstone, down Church Lane. Downhill all the way to the T-junction. Turn right along the A677(T) – with care! Turn left in 200 metres to go up Further Lane. The surroundings are very rural, once more. After about a mile, turn left into the track that begins the bridle-way, marked 'Alum Scar Lane'. Continue along the metalled lane, going straight on and down the path to the wood, off the road that swings right to the farm. Although unmarked, this is an excellent narrow track that leads down towards the river, through the wood, and up the other side on an obvious woodland track. Ride up to a lane, then continue straight on, exiting the fine bridleway and continuing to a T-junction, (see Sustrans NCN).

Turn right, along Billinge End Road on the pleasantly twisting and undulating country road that becomes Woodcock Hill Road, then Long Lane, Sandy Lane and finally, as we pass the Butler's Arms, Victoria Road! Now in a more built-up area. Continue over the railway in Pleasington, past The Railway (pub), and through this attractive village. Down the dip and over the river, past Fennicowles parish church, and on to the end of Pleasington Lane at the T-junction.

i) – j)

Turn right (care!), following the Preston sign, downhill gently, over the river and past the signs 'Chorley, Houghton'. Uphill to the traffic lights, where we turn left along Finnington Lane, following the signs to Chorley and Manchester. Continue down to the new roundabout feeding the M65, taking the third exit and following the sign 'Wheelton, A674'. Past the Houghton Arms and straight on through Higher Wheelton, passing the Golden Lion and Wheelton School (1842). Along the Blackburn Road, past the Wheeler's Arms, following the sign 'Chorley, A674'.

Half a mile further on, turn left into the lane marked 'Heapy, White Coppice', along Chapel Lane. The undulating and winding lane leads to The Railway (pub). Turn left here, down Coppice Lane to White Coppice (the railway track has long gone). Follow the road around a sharp right bend at White Coppice (ignore the track straight on, at the end of which is the most impressively-sited cricket ground in Lancashire, at the start of the West Pennine Moors). We follow the Anglezarke signpost along Hollin Lane to a T-junction. Turn left and along Higher House Lane for a quarter of a mile to Cliff Farm. We turn right here, into the well-marked bridleway to Healey Nab, part of the Rivington route.

j) – k) (as Route 2, e) to b))

Go up the excellent, rugged bridleway, over the rise to follow the obvious track down to the reservoirs. At Heathfold Farm we turn right along the concrete road to the T-junction at the end of the bridleway. Turn left and

Arnside Downham (Pendle beyond)

along Back Lane to the next T-junction; across is the Yew Tree. Turn left
along Knowsley Lane, towards Anglezarke. Over the reservoir, and turn
right on its far side, up the signposted bridleway. Past the weir and right at
the track junction. The good track feeds into the metalled lane, and reaches
a T-junction at Rivington Club. Turn left, then in 50 metres right, into the
marked bridleway that runs past Rivington School, to follow the shore of
Rivington Lower Reservoir. A delightful run amongst the woodland (one
can surely still appreciate such aesthetic appeal, even near the end of this
journey), brings the 'castle ruins' to hand. We turn left, along the impressive avenue that leads past a car park and to the road, departing the Rivington route here.

k) – l)

Turn right, along Lever Park Avenue to Horwich in half a mile. Turn left,
along the main road to the roundabout in under 100 metres, where we fork
left along the B6226. Go straight on for half a mile (and past Victoria Road
on the right), and follow the Barrow Bridge route to the finish.

l) – m) (as Route 1, e) – a))

Past the Black Bull then the Brown Cow, where we turn left into Mill Lane
(leading to Foxholes Road). Keep right at the fork, up the last steep climb,
which winds its way to the T-junction at the top – we're now back to the
edge of Winter Hill. Turn right and along as we contour around the hill,
providing great views over the Lancashire (and Cheshire) plain. Go up a
rise and at the brow turn left, along Matchmoor Lane. A long, slow rise on
this exposed road takes us past the 'Welcome to Smithills Hall and Park'
sign, to a more welcome downhill to the T-junction. Turn left, along the undulating road to Collier's Row and Farm.

In 150 metres, turn right down Longshaw Ford Road. Downhill for 200
metres and turn left into the bridleway. Continue along the good track, easily followed, past the cottages and down to meet Smithills Dean Road. Turn
right and roll down the last couple of hundred metres to Smithills Hall entrance, on the left. Finished at last!

The Bolton mainline railway station is easily reached from the Hall,
simply follow the signs for the centre and station, a couple of miles further
south.

Routes – summary

			(mls.)	*(%)*	*(ft.)*
Ref	*Route*	*Region*	*Distance*	*Off-road*	*Ht. gain*
1	Barrow Bridge	West Pennine Moors	15ml	30%	1050ft
2	Rivington	'	12	72	600
3	Belmont	'	14	31	1300
4	Ramsbottom	'	15	54	1250
5	Whitworth	Central Pennines	12	50	900
6	Hollingworth Lake	'	8	78	850
7	Piethorn Valley	'	15	51	1250
8	Oswaldtwistle	'	10	63	650
9	Huncoat	'	14	36	850
10	Rawtenstall	'	13.75	49	1250
11	Worsthorne	'	21	36	1900
12	Wycoller	'	12	42	1250
13	Ribchester	Ribble Valley	17	59	700
14	Whalley	'	19	21	1050
15	Sawley	'	12	36	550
16	Bolton-by-Bowland	'	18	59	800
17	Barley	Pendle	7.5	58	950
18	Downham	'	20.5	28	1550
19	Chipping	Forest of Bowland	15	25	1350
20	Slaidburn	'	18	45	2500
21	Dunsop Bridge	'	13.75	68	1500
22	Grizedale	Lune Valley	8	39	700
23	Glasson Dock	'	20	38	400
24	Crook O' Lune	'	19	43	1800
25	Burton-in-Kendall	Arnside/Silverdale	25	40	1600
26	Silverdale	'	17	26	1100
27	Arnside – Slaidburn (Day 1)		35	36	3020
	Slaidburn – Smithills Hall (Day 2)		51	27	4150

Routes — Grading

See 'Getting Ready. **Grading:**   Easy, Moderate, Difficult, Severe; : 'A' steepest.
Rating: 'Quality' – 3-stars best.

Route	Grading	Gradient	Rating
Glasson Dock	Easy	C	*
Grizedale	Easy	C	*
Hollingworth Lake	Mod (-)	B	*
Oswaldtwistle	Mod	B	*
Barrow Bridge	Mod	B	*
Silverdale	Mod	B	**
Rivington	Mod	B	***
Belmont	Mod	B	*
Wycoller	Mod	B	*
Worsthorne	Mod	B	*
Whitworth	Mod	B	*
Huncoat	Diff (-)	B	*
Piethorn Valley	Diff (-)	B	**
Whalley	Diff (-)	A	**
Crook o' Lune	Diff (-)	B	**
Ramsbottom	Diff (-)	B	*
Burton-in-Kendal	Diff (-)	B	**
Sawley	Diff	B	-
Chipping	Diff	B	*
Rawtenstall	Diff	A	**
Barley } Downham	Diff	A	***
Ribchester	Diff (+)	B	*
Bolton-by-Bowland	Sev (-)	B	*
Dunsop Bridge } Slaidburn	Sev	A	**
Arnside – Smithills Hall	Sev (long)	B	***

Pedal Power from:

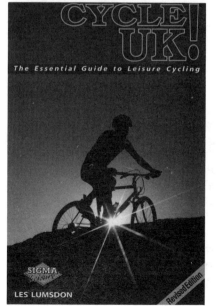

Also by Henry Tindell:

BY-WAY BIKING IN THE CHILTERNS

Henry Tindell travels far and wide for his cycling pleasures. Head south with Henry and discover the joys of cycling in The Chilterns. This is a popular area for cyclists of all abilities and this book describes a wide variety of routes on all types of terrain. Routes follow quiet lanes and off-road tracks.

£6.95

CYCLE UK!
the essential guide to leisure cycling

Les Lumsdon's guidebook is packed with information, sound advice and a handpicked selection of cycle rides for each region. This is the book for everyone with a love of cycling – and especially those who want to venture beyond their own patch.

"Anyone with serious intentions about leisure cycling should have it handy" EVENING SENTINEL (Staffordshire).

£9.95

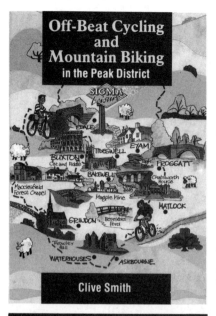